At long last, with a colourful career spanning decades, my dear friend Ronald Chapchuk, a larger than life, award-winning meat purveyor, widely considered the best in the business, has decided to share his personal anecdotes in this unique, Toronto based book of cultural and historic significance!

William Zilinek, MSA Docent Salvador Dali Museum, Florida

———————

After many successful years in the meat business, Ron found he has an astonishing number of colourful stories to tell. With his outgoing and gregarious nature, his energy, he was always able to make fast friends with many interesting people in the Toronto restaurant and hotel business during the better part of the 20th century.

Peter Hackenberger, Hospitality Executive

———————

Ron Chapchuk's look back at eating out in Toronto is delicious nostalgia.

Ed Roman, Photographer

———————

There is not a restaurant or meat shop that has not been blessed by Ronald Chapchuk. His words and experiences are to be treasured.

Walter P. Hryciuk

———————

Dealing for half a century in the meat business, Ron Chapchuk's The Meat Man is 'well done.'

Norman W. Tomas, J.D.

MEAT MAN

Library and Archives Canada Cataloguing in Publication
Chapchuk, Ronald, 1941-, author
    Meat man : an insider's history of Toronto's greatest restaurants
/ Ronald Chapchuk.

Issued in print and electronic formats.
ISBN 978-1-77161-127-5 (pbk.).--ISBN 978-1-77161-128-2 (html).--
ISBN 978-1-77161-129-9 (pdf)

    1. Restaurants--Ontario--Toronto--History--20th century.
2. Restaurants--Ontario--Toronto--Anecdotes. 3. Chapchuk,
Ronald, 1941- --Anecdotes. I. Title.

TX910.C3C43 2014   647.95713'541   C2014-906157-9
                                                      C2014-906158-7

Pubished by Mosaic Press, Oakville, Ontario, Canada, 2015.
Distributed in the United States by Bookmasters (www.bookmasters.com).
Distributed in the U.K. by Gazelle Book Services (www.gazellebookservices.co.uk).

MOSAIC PRESS, Publishers
Copyright © 2015 Ronald Chapchuk

Printed and Bound in Canada.
ISBN Paperback 978-1-77161-127-5
          ePub 978-1-77161-128-2
          ePDF 978-1-77161-129-9

Book layout and design by Eric Normann

We acknowledge the financial support of the Government of Canada through the Canada Book Fund (CBF) for this project.

Nous reconnaissons l'aide financière du gouvernement du Canada par l'entremise du Fonds du livre du Canada (FLC) pour ce projet.

 Canadian Heritage Patrimoine canadien

MOSAIC PRESS
1252 Speers Road, Units 1 & 2
Oakville, Ontario L6L 5N9
phone: (905) 825-2130
info@mosaic-press.com

www.mosaic-press.com

MEAT MAN

An Insider's History of Toronto's
Greatest Restaurants

Ronald
Chapchuk

This book is dedicated to my daughter Robin Anne Marie, who has a very gentle heart and has taught me a lot about hope and courage.

CONTENTS

FOREWORD

This book is not only about some of Toronto's most important restaurants, but about many of the ones that I supplied as a meat purveyor for over five decades, starting in the '60s. I can honestly say that most of my experiences with these restaurants have been very rewarding, and I feel that this book has been something I had to write to fulfill my forty five years in the meat industry. I could have written about a lot of bad things, and although it might be the truth, I would have incriminated, and upset, many people. Obviously, this book would have been much more interesting and dynamic, but it probably would have meant many lawsuits. Most people have been very kind and helpful in providing information. A very few have not, so have a nice day!

Some of the people I mention have become good friends, and others have become good acquaintances. I have built my business on relationships that have served me well, and feel very lucky and honoured to have passed through what is probably the greatest time for restaurants. I have probably missed a few restaurants in this book, so I do apologize to those people. Most of these omissions are due to me never having had any business dealings with them, and I did not want to guess as to what they represented or who they were. The book is divided into sections, most of which are self-explanatory. Two sections, highlighting some of the best restaurants over the last five decades in Toronto, are called 'Jewels' and 'Gems'. I do not place more importance on one category than the other. I simply saw these restaurants fitting into these two groupings. Some places that were truly special and memorable deserved special mention and stand on their own.

I am certainly not a chef or a wine expert by any means, but I have probably eaten and drank the very best. My mother was not a gourmet cook, but we always ate the best that our family could afford. My mother's motto was 'the more you eat, the healthier

Unused proposal for Gay Lea Foods advertising campaign (ca. 1990)

you would be'. Needless to say, I have had a weight problem for most of my life. Being of European extraction, I was told you ate everything on your plate. Bottom line—I love to eat, and so my attention to the food industry, particularly meat, was natural. I felt somewhat embarrassed by inviting certain customers, such as Harry Barberian (owner) and his wife Helen of Barberian's Steakhouse, and Gerhard Neubauer (chef) and his wife Elke, to my house for dinner. Obviously I supplied the meat and cooked it. Christian Vinassac and his wife Elizabeth, owners of Napoléon, the only "five star" restaurant in Canada during the '60s and '70s, came over and we had rib eye steaks; very simple. I have probably cooked thousands of beef steaks, veal, lamb, pork and chicken products, but cannot tell anyone how long it takes to barbeque a certain piece of meat.

Barbeque means different things to different people. To me, barbeque always meant steaks or ribs. When I moved to Florida in the early '70s, we were invited to a Memorial Day barbeque. Great! I brought four wonderfully aged and marbled steaks. To my chagrin, I was the only one with this idea, and everyone thought that I was some kind of Canadian snob. The other guests brought hotdog wieners, sausages and burgers. Flash-forward to today, things have changed dramatically, as totally different cuts of meat, like beef brisket, pork shoulder and pork butt, have taken on new prominence with fans of barbeque. Everyone is now a barbeque 'expert', though how anyone got to this position is beyond me. So many books on barbequing have been written in the last decade, and yet the basic tools and skills to cook meat over a wood fire haven't changed much since the cavemen. In terms of cooking steaks, charcoal, propane, nat-

ural gas and high temperature gas and electric ovens have all been used to create culinary works of art. There are people that say steaks taste the best on charcoal because it brings out the most flavour. However, with some of the cooking tools used now, that point could certainly be disputed.

What is the best restaurant or steakhouse in Toronto? I have been asked that question many times. That is a hard question to answer because it considers the whole experience of going out, and not just the experience of eating a piece of meat. Your day, or your partner's day, may have started out badly and progressed that way. A wait-staffer may not have greeted you, or looked at you, in the proper manner. You may have gotten a bad table. Many other things could have put you off, and thus, no matter how your meal was prepared, it still would not be first class to you. It is the complete dining experience that you must have. Then, and only then, can you determine what the best eating establishment is for you. Attentive service, nice ambiance, great food, and good value for money spent, are all part of it. You may have had a great meal, but if those other factors aren't positive, you will not be happy. Your every visit to a restaurant will be different.

I must give credit to two gentlemen in the meat industry: Barry Honeyman and Joseph Dermastja. Without them, my life in the meat business would never have happened. I knew Barry from my high school days at Royal York Collegiate in Etobicoke. He had started in the business as a teenager, working for Loblaws on the Queensway in the '50s. He progressed and worked for F. G. Bradley Company in Toronto. He became the National Sales Manager. That is where we met again, by chance. I had sold the family tobacco business and was unemployed and in my mid thirties. Barry asked me to join F. G. Bradley, and I did. Shortly after, he started his own company and again asked me to join him, and I did. I worked with Barry until I decided to move out to Florida with my family in the early '70s. That did not work out. My wife and I divorced. I was a very lucky man and got custody of both of my children and returned to Toronto.

Since there was no equity position available for purchase at Honeyman Beef Purveyors, I was again lucky to know Joseph Dermastja, who owned Dermastja's Meat Market at 192 Augusta Avenue in Kensington Market. We hit it off, and the rest is history. We had a lot of luck, good employees, sold great quality and offered excellent service. I brought in some real quality restaurants along with those that Joe was already servicing, and our journey began.

Alfy Goldberg came to us from Belmont Meats (passed away), and Stan Kray came from F. G. Bradley. We grew the company and had an exciting team. My son, Tim, joined me at J.J. Derma Meats in the early '90s and started his career in the meat business. We have all gone our separate ways and have had continued success. Barry, Joe and I have retired. My retirement has given me the time to write this book, which I hope brings good memories to those who read it. Many restaurants do not have a shelf life of longer than 12 years. Those that do survive either put something in the koolaid they serve, or have reinvented themselves.

While I am writing this book, my daughter Robin is undergoing chemotherapy for pancreatic cancer. It is a terrible thing, but she is a tremendous inspiration to me. She keeps me going every day because she knows it is important. She knows I am at her beck and call and the support she is getting from her family, friends and workplace at CAMH, is quite awesome.

Chaîne des Rôtisseurs Medal awarded to Ron Chapchuk.

Escoffier Society 30th anniversary commemorative plate given to Ron Chapchuk.

Chapchuk Family Crest

BABA'S OPEN KITCHEN

In writing this book I was torn between adding this chapter or not. I finally decided that I had to, out of respect for my mother and the legacy that she left for me and my family. My mother, Mary Chapchuk, was called "Baba" by my children and family. "Baba" means grandmother in Ukrainian. Baba was not a gourmet cook, but she knew how to prepare delicious food out of simple recipes, which she learned by trial and error, cookbooks and from friends. She prepared the food to her taste and never wrote down what ingredients she used or how long it took to prepare—it was all in her head, and it stayed there. Friends of hers prepared similar dishes, but they did not taste the same as Baba's food. She had many requests to prepare her favourites for special occasions and she always filled the requests. Her braided egg bread, which is called "Challah" by the Jewish community, is called "Paska" by the Ukrainians. She would bake smaller ones called "Babkas" for the Christmas and Easter holidays. She would bake a dozen of these "Babkas" and give them to friends as gifts. Her annual Christmas cake was quite a project. She had a carpenter make two rectangular pine boxes which measured about 8" x 12". They were fitted together with dado joints and not nailed or glued. They were quite special. Many people never believed that these Christmas cakes were baked in open wooden containers. This cake process started in September when all of the ingredients were bought and mixed together. Buying these ingredients could be quite costly, but it was for Christmas so it was a once a year expense. Ingredients such as raisons, pineapple, lemon peel, orange peel, cherries, corn syrup, sugar, almonds, walnuts, pecans, fancy molasses and many other spices, were used to produce this creation. But the most important additive was the brandy, which my mother would liberally drizzle all over this cake. It would then be baked and put away safely for the Christmas season.

Another dessert she made was called "Krustiki." It was quite simply an egg, vanilla and flour mixture that was cut into with lard, then rolled out and formed into bow-tie pastries. These pastries were then deep fried carefully in Crisco oil, not to be over cooked, and then sprinkled with icing sugar when cooled. Once you started to eat these you could not stop—they were addictive. Her honeycake, upsidedown pineapple cake, assorted cheese cakes, cookies and doughnuts were luscious and were never around very long.

Baba's cabbage rolls were classic. The key to those cabbage rolls was the size of the cabbage. They had to be small and very hard. Baba would go through 30 cabbages before she picked out six. She would drive the produce manager crazy. She never put any meat in them so they could have been called vegetarian. They were rather small in size. The cabbage rolls of today have varying amounts of ground meat in them, to the point where there is more meat than rice. The sizes range from large to very large, and are not too tasty or flavourful. The only place that makes excellent cabbage rolls is Baby Point Lounge on Jane Street—trust me!

Baba's "pyrohy" or "perogies" made from sauerkraut or potatoes and cheese were to die for. She would make perogies filled with blueberries or cherries in the summer, which were not too heavy. Her soups like borscht, potato and chicken noodle, could not be matched by the best of cooks. She always made her own homemade noodles.

Herring was a specialty of hers. I remember we would go to the Jewish market in the '40s and '50s, now called Kensington Market, and she would pick out four large *shmaltz* herrings from a large barrel. She chose female, each with a milk sac in them. She would bring them home, open each one to remove that long sac inside, and then place the herring into a container filled with ice water overnight. The next day each fish would be skinned and deboned very carefully. This was a very tedious and dirty job. The fillets would then be put into olive oil with sliced onions for all to enjoy as an appetizer.

The crowning glory of our Baba's creation was her "Hrein" or horse radish, and how she produced it. She would have to find the hardest and firmest horse radish roots. They were not to be found easily, but once they were, the selection process began in much the same way as the cabbages for the cabbage rolls, or "holobchy." Once home, they were stored in cold water overnight. The next day the soaked roots were dried and skinned. Once that was done the fun began. You had to grate the root. When you started to do that, the vapour would make you cry until you finished. My wife Florence finally had enough of this torture and started using her Cuisinart. That seemed to solve the problem. Red beets would be cooked and grated and then added to the grated horse radish root. A mixture of white vinegar, salt and sugar would be added, and voila! Enough fumes

My mother, Mary "Baba" Chapchuk

to melt a lead pipe. Ukrainians who eat this type of food have been known to live long lives.

The roast beef she prepared was also memorable. It was unthinkable to cook a prime rib roast or serve strip loin or tenderloin. Those words were not in her vocabulary. Baba only bought what was called a wedge-cut rump roast at the local butcher shop, like Hicks Meat Market on Queen Street West or Reisberry Brothers Meats on Park Lawn Road in Etobicoke. It would be cooked to medium well-done, and a thermometer would be sacrilegious to use. With her mushroom gravy and flavourful mashed potatoes, the meal was complete. The only way that I ever ate prime rib was to enjoy it at the Savarin or

Town and Country, where it was served as medium rare. I frequently chose an outside cut as I sometimes do now. This was during the '40s, '50s and early '60s until I learned to appreciate high quality aged and well marbled beef, and became a lover of rare.

Baba's cooking pleased many people. She was never too tired to cook for us and we miss her dearly. We took so much for granted. She was a true "10."

TO DRY-AGE OR NOT TO DRY-AGE

To dry age or not to dry age, that is the question. Fine wine and cheese improve with age; so does properly high grade aged beef. Ageing increases beef tenderness and intensifies flavour. Just look how I have aged! Significant marbling is another key factor in achieving this process. In order for beef to age properly, the refrigerated temperature should be between 33 -36 degrees for an extended period of time. The natural enzymes in the meat break down the proteins within the muscle fibres. Lactic acid accumulates, and the pH of the beef drops. It becomes tender from the accumulation of lactic acid breaking down the protein. This explains why some beef products have a decaying or foul odour to them when the cryovac is opened. If you just leave the product open then you will find that the odour goes away This improves tenderness and creates flavour. These enzymes do their most beneficial work within the first ten days. Supermarket or retail beef is normally aged for five to seven days. That is why you really can't count on a tender steak when you shop at a supermarket, unless they age it for a longer period of time and offer higher quality marbled beef.

Restaurant or food service beef is usually aged longer, from fourteen to twenty one days, and is normally of a higher quality and well marbled. Some wet aged products can survive for 60 to 70 days if under properly controlled temperatures and stored in quality vacuum packaging. Remember, not all beef is aged, but the majority of beef is wet aged. This product is refrigerated in vacuum sealed or cryovac packaging, where all of the air is removed. That is why when you open a vacuum sealed steak, the product will develop a "bloom" and appear more red. That is the introduction of oxygen to the product. Wet ageing maximizes beef flavour and tenderness, but normally does not require any trimming.

Most restaurants use what the trade calls "boxed ready whole muscle product," and trim strip loins, tenderloins, ribs and top sirloin to their needs and required yields. I firmly believe that a lot of steak house beef cuts are over trimmed, but when you are paying premium dollar for a steak dinner, that steak should be perfect in quality and trim. Most restaurants buy their beef products whole and not pre-cut. This way, the chef can cut the product to specification and age the product longer.

Dry ageing is a rare and difficult art. Many restaurants have failed in their attempt to do so. Less than 2% of beef is dry aged. I have been told by steakhouse owners and chefs that they dry age their beef, but when I see their operation they are wrong, because the factors needed for dry ageing are not in place. In dry ageing, fresh beef primal cuts are stored with no packaging in racks in open air cooling. Humidity is kept between 70 to 80%. Temperature and humidity, combined with ultra violet light, controls bacterial growth. In a federally inspected establishment, if this bacterial count goes too high and these stringent dry ageing rules are not followed, the government inspector can close down the operation or plant. Dry aged meat undergoes dehydration. Moisture evaporates from the surface, concentrating on the meat's flavour inside. This meat is carefully trimmed before being cut into steaks. This dehydration can result in a significant final yield loss for the restaurant owner. Leaner beef loses more weight, so is fat good? Dry age losses can occur due to less that strict sanitation, causing mould and spoilage. Also, dry aged beef is usually more expensive because of yield loss trimming and the cost of keeping a dry ageing cooler. Dry ageing gives the meat a more nutty, beefy or roasted flavour that many discerning palates enjoy. Cooking time is reduced with dry ageing. Dry ageing often results in the growth of moulds that contribute their own distinctive flavour. Only a firm well-marbled product should be dry aged.

A Toronto butcher's table laden with fresh cuts of meat and price cards.

CHINATOWN

The front exterior of The Nanking Restaurant.

The front exterior of Lichee Garden (ca. 1970).

The first Chinese restaurant in Toronto opened in 1901 at 37 ½ Queen Street West, and was called Sing Tom's. Chinese food was not served back then the way it is now. Sandwiches, soup and roast beef were the daily fare. Only later, in the 1920s, did menus expand to introduce Chinese culinary dishes. By the early 1920s, Chinese restaurants had congregated to the Elizabeth-Dundas Street area. This area was already known as "Chinatown." As the availability of ingredients pertinent to Chinese cooking became more available and popular, so did the attraction of non-Asian patrons to the Chinese community. Peking (northern), Szechuan/Hunan (south-western), Cantonese (southern), and Shanghai-Fujian (south-eastern) styles of cooking all became very popular, with Cantonese the most popular and Shanghai-Fujian the least popular.

My introduction to Chinatown and Chinese restaurants came when I worked for a company called Swift and Company in the 1960s. I was employed as a salesperson and was given what was designated as the downtown territory. Swift and Company sold a lot of pork products. Thus, I had the main meat products popular in Chinese cuisine. The two main items that I sold to the Chinese restaurants were pork side spare ribs and New York pork shoulders. Lard was used in Chinese cooking as well. These three items were so popular that twice a week, Tuesdays and Fridays, my delivery truck was jam-packed from top to bottom. One truck was designated only for those deliveries. This was a 12' to 14' refrigeration box and this was only for six restaurants in Chinatown. The restaurants I serviced in the 1960s were Golden City, Golden Dragon, Lichee Gardens, Nanking Garden, Kwong Chow and Sai Woo. Holima Gardens was also a very large customer in the East End of Toronto. These restaurants are long gone now and the present establishments are nowhere near the places that once existed. I developed a very good relationship with my favourite Chinese restaurant of all time, Lichee Gardens. They were excellent customers and many of the staff dealt with me when I became a stockbroker with Bache and Company, a member of the New York Stock Exchange in the late 1960's. Sing Soo, one of the partners, and Ken Fong, a waiter, became my good friends and always took care of my family when we visited. We went there on special occasions, like birthdays and anniversaries; it was a place where you felt quite comfortable with your children. They served about 350,000 patrons a year. They prepared over one thousand pounds of shrimp weekly, and grew their own bean sprouts, so they were always fresh. Their cuisine was always delicious. My favourite was the "Moy-Tun Stove," which consisted of BoBo Mongolian beef, fan tail shrimps, barbeque spare ribs, scallop rolls, and Jaa Guy Gwan. This was the appetizer for us. Dinner for two with wine was about twenty-five dollars.

The red and yellow colours of the dining room made for a warm and relaxed atmosphere. Lloyd Burry, who also played piano and organ at the Town and Country, entertained with favourite musical and birthday requests. The banquettes around the side of the main dining room provided privacy if needed, and the large hand drawn paintings on the walls were from Hong Kong.

Kwong Chow at 126 Elizabeth Street, Sai Woo at 123A Dundas Street West, and Nanking Garden behind City Hall, served great lunches and did a very brisk business. Kwong Chow had an entire menu just for Chinese pastries and desserts. Dinner at Sai Woo started around ten dollars and was one of Toronto's greatest bargains in price and excellent cuisine. All of these places served quality, and gave great value for the dollar spent. Needless to say, Chinatown exploded west, north, and east and now Toronto is saturated with Chinese, Thai, Korean, Vietnamese and other Asian-themed restaurants.

Lichee Garden postcard. (ca. 1970).

THE EARLY JAPANESE RESTAURANTS

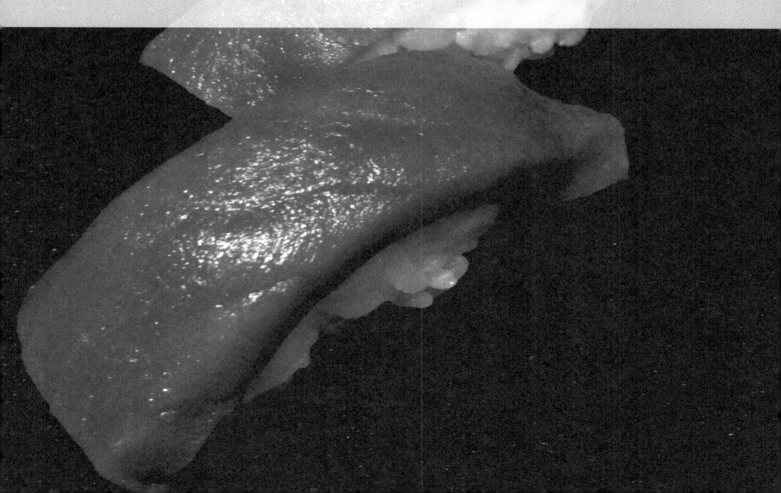

The early Japanese restaurants had a hard time of it when they started in Toronto. They were not like the Chinese establishments, which had a fifty-year head start. This was 'raw' food, which was very slow to catch on. These early Japanese restaurants served authentic dishes where the customers were primarily the same customers who visited frequently. Their menus were predominantly fish, although the Japanese have been known to have the finest beef in the world—called Kobe—which is a province in Japan. Many restaurants advertise that they are using Kobe beef, but that is not true unless it is from Japan. It is more likely to be Wagu, which is raised in the United States or Canada. If it is not raised in the Kobe province it should not be referred to as Kobe.

Nikko Sukiyaki Gardens opened in 1960 at 460 Dundas Street West. It was the first Japanese restaurant in Toronto. It was family friendly and known for its full course meals and variety of dinners. The décor was quiet and subdued. The tables were placed wide apart with rice paper dividers for privacy. The wait staff were very knowledgeable and explained the ingredients in the dishes. A specialty of the house was miso shiru soup made of bean paste and bean cake.

Sushi became extremely popular in the 1970s and just took off. To become a trained sushi chef was a long, arduous job. It was a very unique title that took years to master. Now there seems to be a sushi restaurant on every corner in Toronto. To become a true sushi chef in Japan, you would go through an apprenticeship program that would take many years to complete.

Masa Hara opened Masa in 1977 at 205 Richmond Street West. Previously, he owned a restaurant named Michi, which was named after his wife and incorporated into Masa. Kimono clad butterfly-like waitresses fluttered around the shoeless patrons to faint Japanese music. Fantastic sushi, shrimp, eel, octopus, tempura, and sukiyaki were accompanied by warm sake or cold Japanese beer. Green tea made a great finish for the outstanding cheesecake they served.

Tanaka of Tokyo at 1180 Bay Street was primarily a Teppanyaki place, with fixed price dinners and a much louder atmosphere than the traditional Japanese restaurants. Screens, prints of Japanese scenery and lots of wood gave a comfortable atmosphere, although there was always a lot of activity going on.

The Katsura at the Prince Hotel (900 York Mills) was also a very popular place to go. They had a fixed price dinner, good beef selections and baked clams, shrimp, oyster, scallops and sal-

mon. Here again, it featured a Teppanyaki style. Mr. Uli Herzig was the Executive Chef at the Prince and a good customer for both the hotel and the Katsura.

Of course, my largest Japanese steakhouse customer in the '70s and '80s was the Benihana of Tokyo in the Royal York Hotel. This was a Japanese-American style steak house and not what you would call traditional. They always bought the highest quality US Prime and US choice corn fed beef, as did Katsura. The chefs would always put on a great show cutting up your choice of meat, chicken or seafood. It was like watching a circus performance.

A very honourable mention is in order to Barry Chaim of Edo Japanese Restaurant. When he opened his fabulous restaurant he chose J.J. Derma Meats as one of his major suppliers. I would also like to mention Kunio Ichi, whom I met in the early 1980s at the Hotel Toronto, along with my friend Angelo Fernandes, who was the Executive Chef at the Metropolitan Toronto Convention Centre. Not that I am any kind of an expert, but Ichi probably made some of the best sushi and other Japanese food around. We have dined at one another's homes for traditional Japanese fare. He made the sushi at the Metropolitan Toronto Convention Centre for years and catered my wedding on September 7, 1985. Ichi remains a true friend of the family.

THE GREAT DELIS

Brought up in the Queen and Bathurst neighbourhood, I became a deli freak at a very young age. I was able to enjoy and live through the best delicatessen food there ever was. Within walking distance of my Father's cigar store—The Lucky Strike Cigar Store at 578 Queen Street West—were the best delis in Toronto. There was Switzer's on Spadina, Shopsy's on Spadina, Red Pancers on Dundas, Becker's on College and Coleman's on Dundas. Throw in The Stem Open Kitchen on Queen Street, Barney's Open Kitchen and Deli across the street and the Oak Leaf Steam Bath. You could get a corned beef or pastrami sandwich every day of the week at a different location and not spend more than fifteen minutes walking there from The Lucky Strike.

Switzer's, at 232 Spadina Avenue, was the deli I frequented most. It was my deli of choice, not only because of the corned beef and pastrami, but because they made wonderful meat knishes, chopped liver, great fries in peanut oil, tasty potato salad and coleslaw. New dills, full sours and hot peppers were found on shelves stacked around the restaurant. Switzer's was opened by Ed Switzer in 1946 and

Hy Beck and Mel Wagman of Switzer's Deli (1970s)

was one of the oldest delis in Toronto. I admit that my favourites were 'A Fat Baby on Rye', which was a fatty baby beef (not lean), and a 'Dog on a Moon', which was an all-beef steamed frankfurter on a poppy seed roll. When I grew older and married in the '60s, and later had children in the '70s, my young family and I ventured downtown frequently and enjoyed that great food. We lived in Mississauga then, but were always keen on coming downtown to eat. Ed Switzer retired and sold his business to Hy Beck, who came from Montreal and worked at Levitts Kosher Deli. Bernice was my favourite waitress, who was always upbeat and pleasant. Cherise Beck, now co-owns and operates Switzer's on 7310 Torbram Road, north of the Toronto airport. Mel Wagman became a partner as well, and

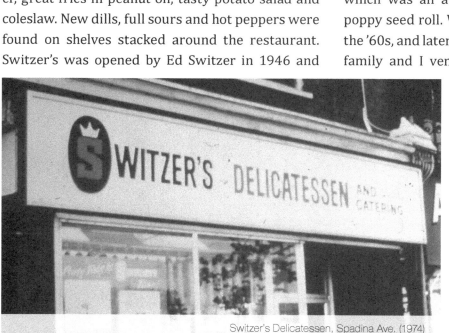

Switzer's Delicatessen, Spadina Ave. (1974)

seemed to be there most of the time. They enjoyed a large catering and take out business, and I remember using their services on a regular basis for all kinds of occasions.

Across the street was Shopsy's Deli, which sat next to the Victory Theatre (which later became a burlesque and strip tease place) at 295 Spadina Ave. The Shopsowitz family, Harry and Jennie, opened Shopsowitz Delicatessen in 1921, which became known as Shopsy's. Both Switzer's and Shopsy's survived even though they were directly opposite each other. At Shopsy's, you could get a hand cut sandwich or one from a slicer. I really did not know which was better, but there was always a long line for the hand cut. Sam Shopsowitz bought U.S. Choice and U.S. Prime beef briskets (fatty and well-marbled) and his advertisements called him the "corned beef King." His place outside the Food Building at the Canadian National Exhibition (CNE) was always packed. My friend Harold Ballard also had a piece of the action at that Shopsy location.

The first day I walked into Red Pancers, I thought I was walking into someone's house. The floor was linoleum and the tables were covered with coloured plastic. There was a large front window, which was steamed up from the heat and steam from the restaurant. I think the price of a corned beef sandwich was fifteen or twenty cents, and the year was 1954.

At Becker's, on College Street, you could order a special spice that you could sprinkle over the meat of your sandwich. It had a distinctive spicy flavour and patrons went there for that. Coleman's also deserves a very honourable mention for their tasy deli food.

Barney's Open Kitchen, at 385 Queen Street West, served the best chili in town and he often served it to you personally. Barney opened and closed by 4 pm daily. A lot of his customers were in the 'shmata', or clothing business, that centred around Spadina Avenue. Their workday began early and ended early. Barney served great French toast and all-day breakfasts, which also became trademarks of his. His fries were also famous be-

Dick Shatto and Lou Agasee at Shopsy's (October, 1961)

The interior of Shopsy's Deli, featuring the meat counter.

Shopsy's booth outside of the food building at the Canadian National Exhibition. (1960s)

The exterior of the front of Shopsy's Deli. (1960s)

cause they were made from scratch, and he also served a superb corned beef sandwich that was hand-cut.

The Stem Open Kitchen was across the street from Barney's on Queen Street West. Barney's was closed on Saturday night, so I ate at The Stem. They made an outstanding corned beef sandwich, although they were mainly known as a diner, along the same lines as The Mars.

The Oak Leaf Steam Baths opened in 1939 on Bathurst Street. It was above Queen Street, about two blocks north of my father's Lucky Strike Cigar Store. You would think, 'What the hell is a steam bath doing serving one of the best corned beef sandwiches in Toronto?' This meat was piled high on a Kaiser bun. The sandwich was so thick that you could not get your mouth around it. This was in the late '50s and the sandwich cost a buck during Friday and Saturdays from about 4 pm until midnight. The two guys that ran the place could not stop because the place was so busy.

now, with really no flavour. It's sad when you have to go to Montreal, to Schwartz's, to get a great sandwich, which they now call 'Montreal Smoked Meat'. In fairness, there are exceptions. I do frequent The Centre Street Deli and like their products. Cheryl Morantz and Sam Agelopoulos came from the Snowden Deli in Montreal and established the busiest and most popular delicatessen in Toronto. They use Lesters Meat from Montreal, my good friend Brian Silverstein's rye bread, and various mustards to add tang. An honourable mention goes to Peter's Fine Dining and Deli on Eglinton Avenue West at Tomken Road for also servimg a good smoked meat sandwich.

One never knew the history behind these restaurants until they closed or were passed along to other owners. They never were the same again because time passed them by. The memories are there, but not the restaurants. As I grow older, I am so happy that I could enjoy and experience those years. I know that readers of my book will certainly disagree as to who made the best sandwich. With all due respect, that is their choice.

Most of the delis processed their own briskets and did their own spicing. This is why the end product was so good. It kills me when I see the products that are produced today that aren't even produced from briskets, but from inside and outside rounds, and imported from other countries that provide cheaper products. There is no quality eating experience. Everyone wants lean-lean-lean

Exterior of the Oak Leaf Steam Baths

CZEHOSKI BUTCHER SHOP

Czehoski played an important part in my early and middle life in the '50s, '60s and '70s. The establishment is now closed and the location, at 678 Queen Street West, is now a restaurant with the original sign 'Czehoski' on the front. In the early days, the Czehoski name in the Polish community was famous. In my opinion they made the best *kielbasa* (Polish) in North America. It was not a ham flavoured *kobassa* (Ukrainian) that most of the other Ukrainian and Polish butcher shops made. Czehoski's *kielbasa* did not need refrigeration like the others. The longer you kept it, the harder it would get. It was like a Jewish salami or pepperoni. My Mother would let it get hard, if I did not eat it, and substitute it for pepperoni in her home made pizzas. I would particularly choose the well-done sausage with the cracked skin. Most people would not choose this because they wanted a perfect, non-cracked skin. This *kielbasa* was made special. It was prepared in a hard wood and sawdust oven and had a barbeque, slightly smoked flavour. It was a succulent, juicy and delicious sausage.

Many kinds of *kobassa* or *kielbasa* were sold throughout the city, but none like this delight. I used to work in my Father's Lucky Strike Cigar Store in the '50s and knew that this wonderful sausage was made on Friday for the weekends, and would be sold out before four o'clock on Saturday. My Mother would always serve this before our main course on Sundays with homemade beet horseradish. It was always served at any parties or celebrations at our house. My Mother made her own *kobassa*, but it was roasted and quite different. It was an excellent homemade sausage, but took a lot of time to prepare, what with the grinding, spicing and stuffing. This was an art that my Mother developed and she was asked to make it many times for special occasions by her friends. 'What a pain in the ass', my Mother would say. She would make it for the family, but did not like to make it for anyone else because of the long process.

I remember my Father giving me ten dollars, which was a lot of money in those 'Nifty-fifties'. Czehoski *kielbasa* sold for under a dollar a pound then. I was told to buy about nine pounds of this sausage and then go across the street to buy two large loaves of rye bread at the Future Bakery. I would always have a few extra bucks, so I would sneak in a half dozen chocolate covered doughnuts for myself. With my purchases in hand, I would make my way over to 578 Queen Street West, two blocks away. I swear I would attract all the stray dogs in the neighbourhood before I got to our store. What a wonderful aroma! Well, my Father and I were hungry and could not stand it any longer. We ate four pounds of that exotic sausage and half of a large loaf of rye bread. With a couple of Cokes—life was good. When we arrived home after midnight on Friday night, my Mother asked, "Where's the *kobassa*?" "Gee, Mom, Dad and I were hungry and ate half of it." Five pounds had to suffice after we ate four pounds. Such was life in the "Good Old Days."

During the late '70s, after my family journey to Florida did not work out, John Czehoski (who inherited the family sausage business and moved to the Queensway in Etobicoke) wanted to sell his famous recipe and business. At the time I had just returned from Florida with my two children and was a little verklempt. I was formally offered to buy this business and I seriously considered making kobassa for the rest of my life. But how could I spend fourteen to sixteen hour days making sausage and operating a business that I knew nothing about? Imagine being the "King of *kielbasa*." Again, 'should-a, could-a, would-a'. Well, I did not bite the *kobassa*. I regretted it many times because the Charney family that bought that business made a lot of money and carried on successfully for many years. It was a family operation again, with a mother, father, son and his wife operation. People in the hundreds would line up on holidays and weekends to buy and eat that marvelous sausage. However, I found an excellent home at J.J. Derma Meats and, again, the rest is history as Harry would say. Czehoski Meat Shop is no longer in business. What a pity! On occasion, I can still taste that magnificent sausage in my mind, but on the other hand I am a lot thinner now.

THE FRENCH
CONNECTIONS

LA CHAUMIERE

La Chaumiere, exterior at 77 Charles St. E (ca. 1960)

Opened in 1939, at 36 Asquith Avenue (it moved to 77 Charles Street East in 1950), La Chaumiere was Toronto's first French restaurant. It was also known as the Red Door. Their trademark was an hors d'oeuvres trolley that had an assortment of over twenty items. As it passed by, you could choose whatever you wanted. Their menu was fairly extensive. You could order Dover sole—which would be deboned in front of you—and a selection of filet mignon entrées, which were the most popular items. This was also a restaurant where you could order calves' liver and sweet breads. Thank you kindly for that. I started to sell to them in the early 1970s, and business carried on until they closed in 1988. Other French style restaurants opened in the '60s and later on La Chaumiere lost its appeal. To their credit, it was open for almost fifty years under different owners.

PLAT DU JOUR

TODAY'S
SPECIAL

COQ AU VIN

$5.95!

LA CHAUMIÈRE
French RESTAURANT

DINNER

Hors d'Oeuvres Chaumière

★　　★　　★

Soupe à l'Oignon — Potage du jour

★　　★　　★

Cuisses de Grenouille Provençale	7.25
Queue de Homard, Beurre Fondant	9.25
Crevettes au Vin	6.95
Dover Sole Sauté Amandine	6.75
Rainbow Trout Sauté Belle Meunière	5.50
Filet de Sole Bonne-Femme	5.25
Truite du Lac Mirabeau	4.95
Chicken à la King	4.95
Omelette au Fromage	4.25
Ris de Veau au Madeira	5.50
Demi Poulet Sauté Chasseur	5.50
Escalope de Veau, Sauce Champignon	6.95
Côtelette d'Agneau Grillé	6.95
Médaillon de Filet, Cabaret Sauce	7.25
Filet Mignon à la Chaumière	8.95
Prime Sirloin Steak Maison	8.95

Pommes de Terre — Légumes

★　　★　　★

Desserts
Fromages Assortis

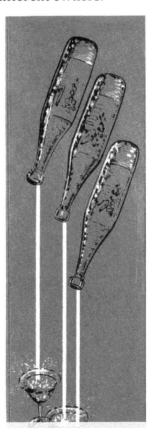

La Chaumiere Dinner Menu (ca. 1970)

LA BODEGA

Philip Wharton opened La Bodega at 30 Baldwin Street in 1979. The restaurant presented very hearty and reasonably priced French food, and the menu was changed daily. The ambiance was very comforting and cozy with the exposed brick walls and lamps, a reminder of Paris's Left Bank. Because the menu changed daily, La Bodega bought a various assortment of meat products and was a place where you could recommend many products. Phillip and his chefs were very innovative and, because of these daily menu changes, used this to their advantage. On the menu, a rack of lamb was priced at $15.00, whereas tenderloin was under $10.00. This establishment became a very good and long-standing customer of J.J. Derma Meats.

LES COPAINS

This French restaurant also became a training ground for many young chefs in Toronto. It was located at 48 Wellington Street East, and enjoyed a very fashionable lunch crowd from the financial district. The dinner crowd came from the theatre, financial district and the very populous bank towers. The sand blasted brick walls, which were adorned with brightly coloured French posters, gave this restaurant a very chic and funky ambiance. There was a good selection of meat and fish on the menu. Traditional French desserts, such as tartes, mousses, crème caramel and sorbets filled out the table d'hôte.

La Provençal Dining Room (ca. 1962)

LE PROVENÇAL

Le Provençal opened in 1962 and became an institution. It was opened by Jacque Ducau, who had previously had a restaurant in the Maritimes, and his experiences there carried over to Le Provençal, where the seafood was carefully chosen and shipped to the restaurant daily. Though labeled a French restaurant, Le Provençal did serve a lot of steak and roast beef. They also became one of my best customers. They presented a very intimate, cozy and tasteful French château atmosphere with their fireplaces, stone floors, wooden beams, tapestries and large candelabras. They had two main rooms: the Rib Room was downstairs and the Hind Quarter was upstairs. In those days, two could have a meal in the Rib Room for $25 - 30 and upstairs in the Hind Quarter for $20-40. Their assortment of foods gave guests a good sampling of the various dishes prepared throughout France. In 1971 a one oz. glass of Louis XIII Cognac went for $5.50 at La Provençal (It now sells for $240!). Beef was predominant on the menu, as was pheasant and quail, and every Tuesday evening a gourmet night was held to feature the chef's culinary skills.

Le Provençal were members of the famous Chaîne des Rôtisseurs, of which I became a member as well. They turned out many young chefs, whom I would later deal with after they finished their apprenticeships. These apprentices included Frank Toneguzzo and Danny Gilbert; two of many apprentices that went on to cook at some pretty fine places. Klaus Mueller later moved to the prestigious Albany Club, and even later to the very popular School of Fine Dining, where he is today. Frank became chef at Le Provençal later on and then moved on to the Albany Club with Klaus. Frank now teaches at George Brown College in the Culinary faculty. Executive chef Theo Lennarts went on to teach at Humber College, and he also served as President of the Toronto Escoffier Society. Danny Gilbert opened his own restaurant in Nobleton, Ontario called Daniel's of Nobleton and was a customer of J.J. Derma Meats for a long time. Danny was also one of the founding members of "Feast of Fields."

LE RENDEZ-VOUS

This restaurant was located at 14 Prince Arthur Avenue across the street from the original Park Plaza Hotel. It had a French décor, combined with a continental motif. Le Rendez-Vous was divided into a series of wood paneled rooms with wood floors. Glass, brass and mirrors made the divided dining rooms very distinct. The menu had a very extensive and assorted selection of meat, including frequent offal choices. The owners were originally from Le Provençal, The Bristol Place, Glossop's and Chez Michel—all restaurants we had previously supplied.

GASTON'S

Gaston Schwalb opened Gaston's at 595 Markham Street in 1964, when "French" became the fashion on the Toronto restaurant scene. I had never tasted bouillabaisse before. My good friend Norman and I were going to a Maple Leaf's hockey game and decided to have dinner at Gaston's first. Norman ordered the large Bouillabaisse as our dinner, and I thought, "why the hell would I come here to only eat soup for dinner?" bouillabaisse was originally made in Provence, France, and was a rich fish stew or soup. It was a combination of seafood—like snapper, eel, lobster, sea bass, fish heads and tails, mussels, scallops—and leeks, herbs, tomatoes, garlic and soup stock. When this large vessel arrived with a ladle, I then realized that Norman was not talking about a bowl of soup. He was talking about a whole meal! With an accompanying loaf of a French baguette, we were stuffed. The bouillabaisse and a few bottles of wine made us want to skip the game and go home to sleep. We did, however, choose to go to the hockey game. Escargot, rabbit and frogs legs were specialties of the house, and garlic certainly did waft generously when you entered the restaurant. Advance reservations were advisable, and Gaston would chauffeur his patrons—if needed—in a yellow Rolls-Royce à la Harry Barberian.

LE TROU NORMAND

Le Trou Normand opened in 1973, at 90 Yorkville Avenue, in the hectic Yorkville area. The owner was Wolfgang Herget, who also became a good friend. I don't think anyone worked harder than Wolfgang, running his own business. As he said, he "played his piano all day long"—meaning his stove. His ever faithful and dedicated assistant, Dalminda, was with Wolfgang through thick or thin. Susur Lee also spent a short time here.

The ambiance changed from lunch to dinner. At lunch the restaurant was bright and busy. In the evening, the mood changed to relaxed and intimate. Obvious touches of Normandy prevailed. Rabbit marinated and served in a prune and gooseberry sauce was a Wolfgang classic. Calvados liqueur was served in the Normandy tradition. The most expensive item here was rack of lamb for two at $17.95, filet mignon with wild mushrooms and herbs was $11.25 and frogs legs in garlic butter with wild mushrooms would set you back $11.25. The restaurant eventually changed hands and was never the same.

I would try to invite Wolfgang and Brigetta to my home many times. It was difficult for them to leave the kitchen a little early to have some late night fun and snacks, or on a Sunday when he might sneak away for a few hours. But one night in the teeming rainfall, when I would not even let my dog out for a moment, Wolfgang and Brigetta dropped by at around 11:00 pm. I lived in Lorne Park (on the border of Oakville) at that time. Here was a guy that was truly a good friend. He came out still dressed in his whites, stayed for a few hours and left at about 1:00 am. What a guy!

HIGH-END PUBS

THE HOP AND GRAPE

The Hop was located at 14 College Street and was opened by Mr. Jorge Berchtold, who had previously owned Le Provençal and other popular restaurants. He later opened Tortilla Flats, one of which was located on Gloucester Street where Fenton's used to be. I would label The Hop and Grape as a high-end British pub. The Hop was very handsomely decorated with plenty of brass and dark wood and was arranged in a series of paneled, separated rooms. This wood paneling was taken from the old Executive office of Eaton's, across the street at the store's College building. Great English-style pub food, such as steak and kidney pie and shepherd's pie were served there. A large selection of roasting meats and steak was always available for your dining pleasure. The staff that had previously made Le Provençal so special ran the kitchen. All kinds of imported and domestic beers and wines were very reasonably priced and made this restaurant a pre and post-game Toronto Maple Leaf hockey favourite dining site.

SIMPSON'S IN THE STRAND

This would certainly not be classified as an English pub, but a very elegantly appointed gentleman's club. This was a reproduction of the original Simpson's-in-the-Strand in London's Savoy Hotel (1848). It was located in the First Canadian Place at Bay and Adelaide. The décor was very traditionally English and all fixtures were imported from England—from the solid dark oak paneling, crystal chandeliers, ornate Chippendale furniture, plush leather sofas and china.

The specialty of the house was roast beef, cut, served table-side from mahogany serving trolleys. It was English cooking at its best by Master Cook Robert Penman, who I believe was the first in Toronto to wear the famous Black Cap instead of white (so soot would not show). Mixed grills, roast lamb, roast duck, steak and kidney pies were also featured. Lunch featured bangers and mash, shepherd's pie and lamb curry. English trifle, creamed rice pudding and poached pears were presented for dessert. A full selection of ales, lagers, fine spirits and wines accompanied this luscious menu. Joe Dermastja from J.J. Derma Meats started to service their meat requirements before I joined him. He must have done one hell of a job because Simpson's in the Strand was quite a discerning organization.

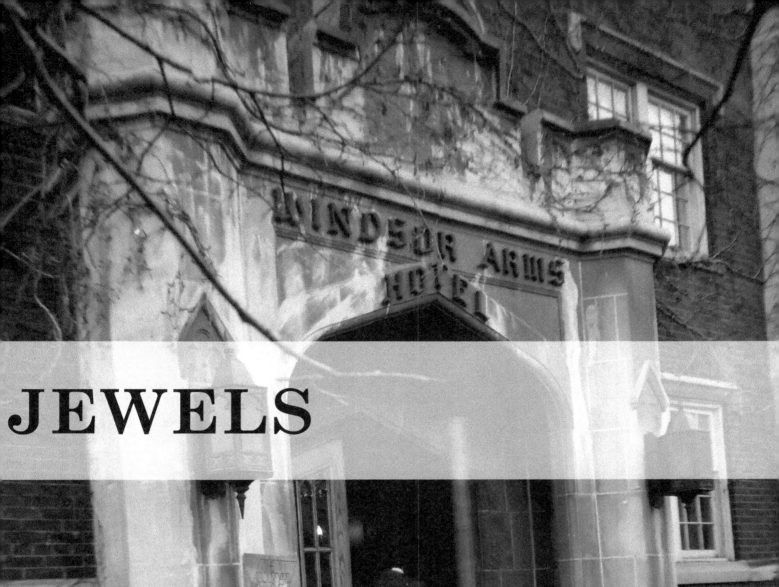

JEWELS

LA CASTILE

La Castile originally opened in 1968. It was destroyed by a major fire on February 23, 1978. Thank goodness no one was hurt. A new structure opened within one year and was much larger. The old La Castile would accommodate about 200 people, and the new about 350. Two brothers owned La Castile, Peter and Ted Triaforos. Together with their families, they grew their business to what it is today. This steakhouse restaurant was the training ground for many waiters and kitchen staff. Many of them have started their own restaurant businesses, much the same as what happened with my friend Harry Barberian's place. Peter and Ted's fingerprints are all over the steakhouse business in Toronto and the GTA. La Castile was sold, but had a short life under some investors from Montreal. In the meantime, Ted and Peter opened up a lovely place called Topiary's, west of the Woodbine Racetrack, which they owned until 1994. George Danos bought Topiary's and owned and managed it. Then Ted and Peter bought La Castile back from the bank and ran it once again. Peter retired from the business in 2006. Ted and his family took over; his wife Sandra, and their three lovely, married daughters Helen, Stacy and Fay, are there today doing marvellous.

La Castile has a very expensive and varied menu ranging from a multitude of steaks, fish, seafood, dessert and flaming coffees. Portions are large but you get what you pay for. The seafood platter is probably the best buy in the house. It could probably feed three or four people because it has Alaska king crab legs, lobster tails, scampi, scallops, a fish selection, and 2-6 oz. filet mignons. Ted has always used the best, well-aged, graded US choice and prime beef and is quite discriminating. Nothing gets by him because he is the man who cuts and trims the day's steaks every morning. He still uses charcoal, and it is amazing to watch him when he gets busy and is grilling one hundred or more steaks at the same time. He looks like he is conducting the Toronto Symphony Orchestra. Inside, the ambiance is like a castle, very palatial, but very comfortable. The family reinvests into the business every year so that the place looks grand and up to date, and there is nightly entertainment in the bar, which is very popular and renowned.

I have been privileged to get to know every waiter in the place, and Ted and Peter and their families have placed a lot of trust in me; I have almost become a member of their family. I have always said that when I retired I would take over the valet parking for that gigantic parking lot. He would have to supply the uniform.

It is known that La Castile has three sittings on New Year's Eve and Valentine's Day, and serves over 800 meals on those two occasions. We are in attendance. In my opinion, La Castile has been known to have the best pork back ribs in the city.

IT'S NOT ALWAYS hot fighting a fire as ice-coated firefighter Campbell Kerr can tell you. He and fellow firemen were on the scene of a blaze that ripped through the 148-year-old Mississauga restaurant, La Castile, yesterday. The fire left the owners with close to a $2 million loss as little insurance was carried. The five-hour blaze also destroyed more than $100,000 worth of paintings. The restaurant was at Dundas Street and Hwy. 427.

Newspaper report of La Castille fire (23, February 1978)

The exteriors of Ed's Warehouse and Ed's Seafood side-by-side.

Toronto's Favorite Restaurant of 1970

As selected by the readers of Toronto Calendar Magazine

the more than ten thousand ballots submitted by Toronto Calendar ine's readers, ED'S WAREHOUSE was chosen as their Favorite urant of 1970. Above, Ed's Warehouse owner Ed Mirvish proudly s the scroll presented to him by Toronto Calendar Magazine on of its readers.

ED'S WAREHOUSE

Ed's Warehouse opened at 270 King Street West and Duncan Street in the early 1960s, and was owned by the King of merchandising, Honest Ed Mervish. For a restaurant that took no reservations, this place was filled day and night. Ed had a very stringent dress code. You had to wear a tie and a sport jacket or suit to enter and be served. It did not matter who you were, that was the code. Ed had an assortment of ties and jackets, not necessarily matching, and you could borrow either or both to sit down to your meal. You were not allowed to wear blue jeans either. This was a beef place that mostly served roast beef, mashed potatoes, and peas. Ed's bought their prime ribs and steak from Benny Winbaum at Vaunclair Packers, the same person that started out with Harry Barberian. As a matter of fact, Harry set up the menu for Mr. Mirvish. Ed Mirvish said it took Harry ten minutes to teach him the restaurant business. Only later in the '70s did I get a chance to sell to Ed. This was a huge account that bought only high quality choice beef products. Because each prime rib had seven bones and the average roast beef portion was six to eight ounces, Ed had to figure out what to do with those bones. Management put their heads together and figured that they would sell those meaty rib bones for lunch. They put three meaty bones on each serving with mashed potatoes and peas and were sold out every day. No waste. What a merchandising achievement! The office buildings on King Street and the surrounding area provided the lunch time traffic. Bus tours, birthdays, anniversaries and other special occasions kept this place hopping. At dinner, it was the pre-theatre crowd that filled the place. It was also very family friendly.

Ed's was truly a highly ornate emporium, with stained glass fixtures, red carpets and antiques. He did own the Royal Alex, so there were many pictures of the performers and celebrities that he hung on the walls of the restaurant. As time passed, he opened seafood, Chinese and Italian restaurants. I was surprised he did not open an old fashioned delicatessen. It would have been a smash hit, but I guess he had his hands full and respected his friends in the deli business. He could have been the mayor of Toronto at any time. His chef and very close friend, Yale Simpson, whom he knew since his high school days, always treated their suppliers with respect and paid their bills on time. I was truly happy to have been a supplier to this restaurant.

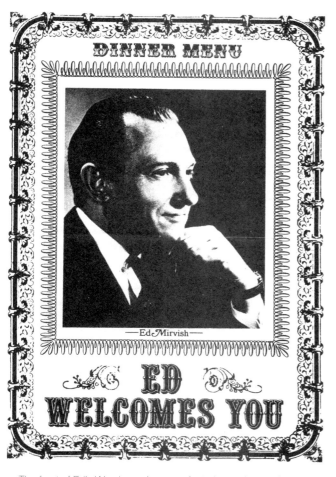

The front of Ed's Warehouse's menu, featuring a picture of Ed Mirvish and an interior page from the menu. (c. 1970)

ED'S WAREHOUSE

Appetizers

Tomato Juice	.50
Salad with our famous warehouse dressing	1.75
French Onion Soup	1.75
Shrimp Cocktail	3.95

Roast Beef

ED'S SPECIAL ROAST BEEF PLATE	5.95
Ed's Favourite	
THE CHEF'S CUT	6.95
A serving of tender, juicy, superb roast beef done to perfection	
THE ENGLISH CUT	7.95
Deftly carved in slices to enhance the rich, beefy goodness	
THE "HONEST ED" CUT	8.95
A tradition since 1966	
THE WAREHOUSE CUT	9.95
A King Size Portion	

Served with mashed potatoes, tender green peas, Yorkshire pudding, delicious kosher dills, fresh rolls and fresh creamery butter.

Steaks

SIRLOIN STEAK NEW YORK CUT, 6 oz	5.95
Ed's delight	
SIRLOIN STEAK NEW YORK CUT, 8 oz	6.95
Chef's Choice	
RIB STEAK, 12 oz.	7.95
Tender and delicious	
SIRLOIN STEAK NEW YORK CUT, 11 oz	8.95
Ed's finest	
FILET MIGNON — BACON WRAPPED, 9 oz	9.95
The One and Only	

Served with mashed potatoes, tender green peas, mushrooms, french fried onion rings, delicious kosher dills, fresh rolls and fresh creamery butter.

Desserts

Ice Cream — Vanilla, Chocolate, Spumoni	.75
Apple Pie with Ice Cream	1.50
Black Forest Cake	1.50
Cherry Cheese Cake	1.50
Chocolate Bavarian	1.50
Carrot Cake	1.50
Pecan Pie	1.50

Beverages

Coffee	.50	Milk	.50
Orange Pekoe Tea	.50	Soft Drinks	.50

Minimum Food Charge 5.95 Per Person

Fully licenced. Reservations for parties of 20 or more please call (416) 593-4466
Ed's Warehouse Restaurants, 270 King St. W., Toronto, Ont., Canada (416) 593-6676

THE WORLD FAMOUS TOWN AND COUNTRY

The world famous Town and Country buffet was a landmark eating destination in the '50s and '60s in Toronto. It was located in the Westminster Hotel on Jarvis Street and Gould. It had no relationship to the present day restaurants that have the same name. The Town and Country presented a lavish display of seafood (lobster and shrimp), various delicious salads, assorted cold meats and some of the best roast prime rib beef in Toronto. The Town and Country was certainly a very worthy competitor to the Savarin. The chef, named Pierre, was not French but of Polish extraction; what a revelation! While a student of Ryerson, I seized any opportunity to dine there. Any guests that visited Toronto were invariably asked if they wanted to visit the Town and Country to eat. When Ed Sullivan hosted the CNE Grandstand Show in the mid-'50s, he took the many dancers there for a treat. My wife Florence was a member of the dancing 'Canadettes' and remembers that treat to this day.

Ed Sullivan headlined at the Canadian National Exhibition with the Canadettes. (left to right) Florence Kundel-Werbny, Ed Sullivan, and Sheila Billings, Miss Toronto. (1956)

LA SCALA

La Scala, housed in a 90 year old mansion, was opened in 1962 and was located at 1121 Bay at the corner of Charles street. It was owned by a father and son—John Grieco the father, and Charles Grieco, the son. It was an instant triumph, which offered a northern Italian bill of fare. The food was superbly prepared in an opulent decor and was brilliantly served to the background music of a harp. The service was impeccable, with reservations a necessity at all times. Waiters were exceptionally trained and very knowledgeable in Italian fare. They also had an after-theatre menu. Green lasagna was a specialty of the house. Their veal piccata romana, scallopine marsala and pizziala were to die for. La Scala was one of Tony Bennett's favourite places whenever he was in town.

This establishment only bought the finest quality of milk fed veal and corn fed US choice beef consistently. To be a supplier to this grand and majestic establishment made me feel so proud. Flambé was a speciality of the house. Flambé is now hardly existent because of fire and insurance regulations. This place became an instant Conservative party hangout and refuge. Winstons and La Scala were the two favourite lunch meeting places of the Queen's Park Conservatives.

If I were to rate the best Caesar salad of that time, it would have to be the one at La Scala. Watching the waiter make it was worth the price of the whole meal. Caesar salad was originated at Caesar Cardini's, an Italian restaurant in the 1920s in Tijuana, Mexico. A war breaks out every time I mention who had the best Caesar salad, and who has the best Caesar now. Not wanting to make enemies at my age, I will not offer my rankings on who makes the best Caesar salad.

Savarin, exterior (1972)

THE SAVARIN

The Savarin is known to most people as a sweet dessert made of rich yeast moulded in a ring shape, but to me the Savarin was a sumptuous buffet restaurant upstairs at 336 Bay Street below Queen Street West at Adelaide. The colourful one hundred foot hot and cold buffet provided a fabulous food show for patrons during lunch and dinner hours. There was a tavern on the lower street level. It was built in 1928 and was popular for fifty years. Edward Assaf was the owner. When I was a teenager I saved my money to go there with my friend Eugene to seriously eat, and I loved to eat. That's why I was overweight in my teenage years. I used to dream of the roast beef and mashed potatoes and all of the fancy salads that I could eat. Of course, I would always eat way too much and the streetcar ride home on Queen Street to the Humber loop was murder. After a triple bromo things sort of worked out and settled down until the next time. After I was married, I took my wife and parents there frequently. The Savarin closed in 1980 for redevelopment. The facade was reconstructed in an enclosed courtyard in the Northern Ontario building at the north west corner of Bay and Adelaide Streets in 1982.

• Thanksgiving Dinner •

1954

Appetizers

Half Dozen Oysters on Half Shell	1.00	Lobster Cocktail	.60
Holland Herring and Onions	.40	Shrimp Cocktail	.60
Oyster Cocktail	.60	Clam Chowder	.30
Anchovies with Olives	.50	Oyster Stew	.85

Full Course Dinners

Celery and Olives or Fruit Cup
Choice of
Tomato, Orange, Grapefruit Juice or Cream of Chicken Soup

$3.75

Broiled Whole Live Lobster with Drawn Butter
Broiled Filet Mignon with Sauted Mushrooms
Broiled Sirloin Steak with French Fried Onions

$2.50

Lobster a la Newburg en Casserole
Roast Prime Ribs of Red Brand Beef (Extra Thick Cut) au Jus
Roast Select Ontario Turkey with Savory Dressing and Cranberry Sauce

$2.00

Baked Virginia Ham with Candied Yams
Fried Breaded Jumbo Shrimps with Tartare Sauce
Fried Breaded Deep Sea Scallops with Tartare Sauce
Fried Breaded Bluepoint Oysters with Tartare Sauce
Broiled Fresh Lake Trout with Lemon Butter

Chef's Salad

Mashed or Au Gratin Potatoes

Choice of
Hubbard Squash   Garden Peas   Pickled Beets

Desserts

English Plum Pudding with Wine Sauce   Cup Custard
French Chocolate Sundae
Assorted Flavours of Ice Cream with Cake   Fruit Jelly with Whipped Cream
Honey Dew Melon   Hot Mince Pie   Pumpkin Pie   Dutch Apple Pie

Oka, Swiss, Danish Blue or Black Diamond Cheddar Cheese with Crackers

Coffee   Tea   Milk

Joso's owner, Joso Spralja

Interior of Joso's dining room and bar

JOSO'S

Joso's was opened in 1967 at 71 Yorkville Avenue by Joso and his wife Angiolina Spralja. It began as a coffee house. They served coffee house type food—which were mainly sandwiches and pastries—but the menu was later augmented by exotic seafood, such as calamari and grilled octopus. Joso was a folksinger of Croatian origin that met another folksinger named Malka Marom. They joined to form a popular duet called 'Malka and Joso', who had their own CBC television show that was featured on Saturday nights after the Toronto Maple Leafs' hockey game.

Their original location was dissolved in the mid 1970s and 71 Yorkville would disappear. Joso and his wife had to make a major decision in their life. Their seafood became so popular with patrons that they had to move to a larger location at 202 Davenport Road. It was here that they built their reputation. They would bring the selections of fish to your table so you could see it, choose it, and then have it cooked and served to your individual taste. They certainly served the best, and freshest, fish in town. Sea bass was available there before it became so popular years later. Daily specials would be featured according to availability. Squid, octopus, mussels and clams were all specialties. There was always a succulent tenderloin steak on the menu.

Sculptures and paintings of large breasted women adorned the restaurant, both inside and out, as did sketches on the menus. A very appealing and seductive atmosphere made this place very popular to visiting celebrities, and reservations were needed in advance. Joso's have never advertised much because their customers come by word of mouth. The restaurant is currently owned by Leo and Shirley Spralja, the son and daughter-in-law of Joso. Their son Marko and daughter Olivia are also involved in the restaurant. As of this writing, Joso is alive and well at 83 years of age living in Zadar, Croatia. Joso was not only a trained opera singer, but a photographer, sculptor, painter and culinary adventurer. His wife Angiolina passed away in 2012.

Joso's outdoor patio

FENTON'S

Fenton's was opened in the summer of 1976 at 12 Gloucester Street, and was a hit from day one. I would drop in after six o'clock. and, by then, the Food Shop was sold out of most prepared items. The building was an older structure, which had previously been a French Canadian restaurant, giving Fenton's somewhat of a head start in terms of aura. The restaurant was decorated daily with expensive and magnificent fresh, exotic flowers. Along with the natural old brick walls, fine china and stemware, it looked like something right out of a French movie.

Fenton's was owned by David Barette and Nicholas Pearce. They were associated with The Windsor Arms, Three Small Rooms, The Four Seasons, The Inn on the Park, The Prince of Wales in Niagara on the Lake and Noodles. The Chef at Fenton's was the very young, but extremely talented, Werner Bassen, who also worked at the Prince of Wales. His was probably the most original menu in Canada. I also worked very closely with a gentleman named Emanuel, who was the 'Jack-of-all-trades'. The two most expensive menu items were a grilled filet mignon (tenderloin) at $14.00, and poached fresh Dover sole with shrimps and scallops served with a lobster sauce at $16.50.

I broke the law on many occasions for this restaurant. They served delicious seafood sausage, which they poached. It was made of shrimp, lobster, scallops and other seafood. I would pick up the seafood sausage mixture in the afternoon to be stuffed early morning and delivered early morning. Our new plant was in the process of becoming Federally Government Inspected. HACCP (Hazard Analysis Critical Control Point) was not yet required. In a Federal establishment, you could not bring in any fresh seafood to produce sausage. It would be acceptable if you were not a Federal plant. This sausage would have to be made and delivered quickly by our sausage maker to guarantee maximum freshness. If an inspector saw this, he could close the plant or deny us getting Federal Government Inspection. It was a dicey game we played, but it was something we as a company had to risk.

I would label Fenton's as a high maintenance establishment, because to do business with this organization you had to be able to deliver two and three times a day from morning to evening. Many times, I would get a call to deliver after hours because Fenton's was so busy for dinner. Werner never used frozen products. I would get into my car—sometimes with my wife, Florence—and deliver after nine or ten o'clock in the evening. A nice glass of wine or cocktail would be waiting for me, and I enjoyed the times I was called upon to deliver. Everyone there became my good friend, as well as business acquaintants. Sadly, in 1989, the restaurant was sold and a year later it closed.

WINSTON'S

The past political personality that I revere most, and eagerly read, is Winston Churchill. Because of this fact, Winston's restaurant has a very special place in my heart. Although Churchill never visited his namesake restaurant, his daughter Sarah did frequently. She visited Toronto in December of 1949, while performing at the Royal Alexandra Theatre in *The Philadelphia Story*. The restaurant was originally established in 1938 by Oscar and Cornelia Berceller, and was located at 120 King Street West. Opened as a diner, and named after Sir Winston Churchill, the name was chosen because there was a sense of 'Anglophilia' in those times and few names were more known than the famous PM and war-hero. As time passed, the Bercellers expanded their menu from diner to a very fancy restaurant, thus attracting a much different, celebrity-type crowd. It became a theatre grill, as well as catering to a celebrity luncheon and dinner crowd.

Winston's celebrity reputation declined in the early 1960s. New restaurants opened, and Winston's became tired, as many restaurants do. Winston's was sold to a group of businessmen and almost went bankrupt. Thankfully, John Arena came to the rescue from the Rosedale Golf Club. John reinvented Winston's into a lunch destination of the power brokers and business elite in 1967. Mr. Arena promoted Winston's to the max. So much so, that the restaurant became extremely successful. In 1973, the area was doomed for redevelopment, and he moved the establishment to 104 Adelaide Street West. John became the ultimate host for his customers and Winston's quickly became the home to establishment-politicians and businessmen who made the most important decisions in Toronto. This restaurant did not have an empty seat in over ten years. French service, but with continental style, nothing was prepared ahead of time; everything was à la minute. Mr. Arena approached each customer, and devoted his life to excellence in dining. During its time, it was probably the most successful restaurant in Toronto. As a sign of its excellence, Winston's achieved a five-star rating, along with Napoléon and the Westbury Hotel.

I happened to be a major supplier to Winston's and was thankful to Mr. Arena, and his two chefs (Peter Colberg and Rolph Romberg), who orchestrated the menu to feature five beef tenderloin items and three milk-fed veal items. Winston's was also the first to serve pâté in Toronto. Thank goodness that seafood and fish were not as popular as the meat entrées, but as time went on, they gained favour. Thank you kindly! But again, history repeated itself. Winston's popularity declined after John sold the restaurant, and it never regained the popularity that it once enjoyed. What a sad scenario for Mr. Arena. The restaurant was torn down again and all those glorious years became only a memory.

WINSTON'S

HORS D'OEUVRES

CREVETTES LINDI, SPÉCIALITÉ DE LA MAISON
Shrimps wrapped in fillet of Dover Sole, a Specialty of the House

COCKTAIL DE CREVETTES
Shrimp cocktail, chilled

CAVIAR FRAIS GARNI
Fresh Caviar Garnished

POIRE ALLIGATOR GARNIE DE CREVETTES
Avocado pear with Shrimps

HUÎTRES FRAÎCHES SERVIES SUR COQUILLE EN SAISON
Fresh oysters, served in the shell (in season)

MOULES À L'ITALIENNE EN SAISON
Mussels with finely-chopped tomatoes, chives and oregano (in season)

COQUILLE ST-JACQUES
Scallops, mushrooms and cream sauce

SAUMON FRAIS À LA SUÉDOISE AVEC SAUCE DILL
Fresh salmon Swedish-style, with dill sauce

POTAGES

CONSOMMÉ DU JOUR
Consommé of the Day

POTAGE DU JOUR
Soup of the Day

CRÈME CRESSONNIÈRE DE MON AMIE CARMEN
Cream of watercress Carmen

CRÈME VICHYSSOISE GLACÉE
Chilled cream of Vichyssoise

TORTUE CLAIRE THÉODORE AU SHERRY
Clear turtle soup with sherry Theodore

SOUPE À L'OIGNON GRATINÉE
Onion soup au gratin

SALADES

SALADE SPÉCIALE WINSTON'S
Heart of romaine, endives, avocado and palm hearts

ENDIVES DE BELGIQUE AVEC VINAIGRETTE
Belgian endives with vinaigrette

SALADE ASCOT
Heart of romaine with fresh orange slices, oil and vinegar

POISSONS

SOLE ANGLAISE POCHÉE "DARLING"
Poached whole Dover Sole "Darling" with cream sauce, lobster and brandy

FILET DE SOLE ANGLAISE BONNE FEMME
Fillet of Dover Sole Bonne Femme, with cream and mushrooms

FILET DE SOLE À L'INDIENNE
Sole with shallots, shrimp, apple, white wine & curry

TRUITE À LA NORVÉGIENNE
Fresh Trout stuffed with Mousse of Pike, Shrimp, Cream, White Dry Wine and Lobster Sauce

HOMARD SERVI AVEC BEURRE FONDU
Steamed lobster served with melted butter (Priced according to size)

ENTRÉES

SUPRÊME DE VOLAILLE—SPÉCIALITÉ DE LA MAISON
Chicken suprême with shallots, pernod and calvados

CANETON DU LAC DE BROME MONTMORENCY
Brome Lake duckling with black cherries and cherry brandy

GIBIER SPÉCIAL DU JOUR
Chef's suggestion for the day "Game with wild rice"

FILET DE VEAU OSCAR
Fillet of veal with lobster, mushrooms, shallots and white wine

FILET DE VEAU MARCIA
Veal with a thin slice of ham, cheese and blanched tomatoes

VEAU ORLOFF
Loin of Veal, Creamed Onions, White Dry Wine, Mushrooms and Truffles
~ served for two ~

CARRÉ D'AGNEAU AUX AROMATES
Rack of lamb, served with white asparagus, cherry tomatoes and snow peas

ENTRECÔTE GRILLÉE
Grilled Sirloin Steak (12 oz)

FILET MIGNON AVEC SAUCE BÉARNAISE
Grilled filet mignon with béarnaise sauce

FILET DE BOEUF WELLINGTON
Fillet of beef wrapped in fine pastry, with périgorde sauce (for two)

CHÂTEAUBRIAND GARNI
Grilled, garnished double fillet of beef (for two)

FILET DE BOEUF FARCI AUX HUÎTRES
Filet mignon stuffed with fresh oysters

TOURNEDOS ROSSINI
Crown of Filet of Beef ~ on a crust ~ served with Foie Gras, and Truffles

DESSERTS

SOUFFLÉ AU GRAND MARNIER
Souffle with Grand Marnier sauce (45 minutes)

BAGATELLE ANGLAISE AUX FRUITS FRAIS
English trifle with fresh fruits, port wine, roasted almonds and cream

FRAISES HAGA
Strawberries, orange rind & Grand Marnier

GÂTEAU FORÊT NOIRE, CHOCOLAT ET CRÈME
Black Forest cake with chocolate, cream and cherries

BOUQUET DE FROMAGES
Selection of cheeses

CRÊPES SUZETTES FLAMBÉES
Paper-thin pancakes and orange sauce, with cognac and Grand Marnier (for two)

CRÊPES ERIKA
Thin pancake, peaches, cream & Port Wine

SORBET DE FRUITS WINSTON'S
Fresh fruit sherbet Winston's

ZABAYON AU CHAMPAGNE ET AUX FRAISES
Zabaglione with champagne and strawberries

SURPRISE À L'ORANGE BONNE COMPAGNIE
Orange slices with almonds, Kirsch and cream

Windsor Arms Hotel, 22 St. Thomas Street (ca. 1974-75)

WINDSOR ARMS HOTEL

This hotel probably rated as Toronto's best small boutique hotel. It has had quite a history. Many chefs and corporate hospitality personnel, with quite eclectic personalities, have passed through this establishment. People like George Minden, George Gurnon, Herbert Sonsogni, Dante Rota, Peter Colberg, Michael Bonacini, Jean Pierre Challet and Anthony Walsh (both later), Freddy LoCicero (who probably could have been a stand up comic), Frank Faigaux, David Barette and Nicolas Pearce. I'm positive that I have missed a few people and I apologize for that.

The Windsor Arms had four restaurants within the hotel: the Courtyard Cafe, and the three small rooms that made up "The Restaurant," "The Grill," and "The Wine Cellar." They were all elegant, but still distinct from one another. Half of the wines offered were private imports. George Minden, at twenty-nine years of age in 1965, designed the three rooms. He was also the importer of Aston Martin automobiles for Eastern Canada. The three small rooms were opened in '65 with "The Restaurant" being the flagship of the hotel. The restaurant served such specialities as duck liver, partridge and Dover sole. The cream soups and sauces were outstanding. No roast beef and Yorkshire pudding served here! The Black Forest cake was some of the best in the city, and the other desserts were bombastic!

The Wine Cellar became a place to be seen as well. It had Scandinavian decor and served marvelous cheeses, cold cuts and small steaks. Wine was served in balloon glasses. The grill featured a meat and seafood menu that changed frequently. This was a busy place, yet very cosy. When you walked out on snow covered 22 St. Thomas street in the winter, you would think you were in an old English movie.

PUSATERI'S

Cosimo Pusateri opened Pusateri's Fine Foods in 1986 at Avenue Road, one block North of Lawrence Avenue. Cosimo succumbed to cancer in 1995, but the tradition of offering the highest quality of food products and services has been carried on to this day.

I have been very fortunate in doing business with them for the last twenty years. They have their own excellent beef aging program and use predominantly Canadian beef product. They've bought, and still continue to buy, top U.S. Choice and U.S. prime corn fed beef from the mid-west. Recently, they have started to purchase U.S. free-range, natural and Halal lamb as well.

Pusateri's was the first to bring in Kobe beef directly from the province of Kobe in Japan. They would usually pre-sell this Kobe product to customers before it arrived. Kobe beef has rarely been available in Canada, so the Wagu breed that Kobe comes from is sourced from Canada, the United States, or Australia. Kobe is a very misrepresented brand and unless it originates from the province of Kobe, it is not Kobe. Restaurants have used the term 'fraudulently', however, people believe them. Joe Figliomeni—Pusateri's Master Butcher—has innovated, at the retail level, the bone-in tenderloin steak, and the Tomahawk Frenched bone-in rib steak, which have become very popular in the steakhouse trade. I mention Pusateri's even though it is a retail account because of the great products they sell, and the professional way they have carried on business over the years.

NAPOLÉON

Napoléon opened in 1969, but I met Christian Vinassac and his wife Elizabeth in the early '70s. Their restaurant was located at 79 Grenville Street, across the street from the Women's College Hospital. Christian would shop in the mornings at the Kensington Market to buy the freshest ingredients for his dinner carte du jour. Fresh flowers were delivered daily, and Elizabeth would arrange them in a glamorous and elegant fashion. Napoléonic artefacts and pictures could be found throughout the dining room, which took on the appearance of a small museum. The old and pleasing home and dining salon held twenty eight guests at each sitting. There were two sittings each evening, with the exception of Sundays and all of August when Napoléon was closed. The restaurant was not opened for lunch. Christian would frequently be out in the dining room conversing with the guests. There was a menu, but Christian would prepare whatever guests decided on. His kitchen was very small, usually being manned by no more than two apprentices and a dishwasher. He was a very charming, low-key man, who was very accommodating. I would say he was just as much of a culinary artist as a master chef. He was a master with attention to detail. His major food preparation would be done in the afternoon, such as his famous lamb paté and his signature rose-formed butter, which was Napoléon's wife Josephine Bonaparte's favourite flower. He made a sweet bread terrine with port aspic, and it was sold out every night that it was offered. I had my first taste of sweetbreads here, although I sold them to other restaurants. They were a difficult

Christian Vinassac, Napoléon owner and chef (ca. 1960s)

item to buy because their shelf life was about forty-eight hours, and because each milk-fed veal animal only had about four ounces. It would not keep, and had to be cooked à la minute and served without delay.

I developed a good personal and business friendship with Christian and Elizabeth, and was very fortunate to provide them with a lot of their meat products. Beef tenderloin, lamb racks and veal tenderloin were all well represented. Pheasant and duck were a speciality, along with certain fish and seafood. However, interestingly, the most expensive meat item on the menu was rack of lamb at $25.50 (carré d'agneau façon du chef). Although Christian was originally from Tunisia, and I believe he lives there now, he preferred simple food. One of his favourites was roasted chicken and frites. He would invite me for lunch, although, as I mentioned, his restaurant was not opened for lunch. The couscous, various snail recipes and other meals he would prepare for our lunches were always fabulous.

The Vinassacs were guests in my home, and a more gracious couple you could not ask for. The French wines they served were remarkable and exceptional. I must tell a story about a gourmet meal that Christian cooked for me. My wife and I were members of a gourmet group of four couples, wherein each month one couple had to host a very special dining experience. When it came to our turn, I was at a complete loss as to what to serve. It had to be extra special because of my involvement in the meat business, but it was not to be just a barbeque. I went to Christian and asked if he could prepare a special gourmet dinner for me. All my wife would have to do is put it into the oven and warm it up. I felt guilty, but "c'est la vie." It was worth it! I would probably admit this sometime later and we would all have a good laugh. Well the guests came, had cocktails, and then the meal was served, and what a great experience! I remember it wasn't anything to do with meat; it was a shrimp and lobster curry with rice and an accompanying salad. It was to die for! I will never forget it because many chefs would not have done that.

Napoléon was the only five star restaurant in Canada in the 1970s (Winston's soon followed with a five star ranking). I remember taking my best friends, Norman and Diane Tomas, for a New Year's Eve dinner there and it was probably one of our most memorable dining experiences to this day, some forty odd years later. Despite all the successes the restaurant had, Napoléon closed in 1984 after a very mysterious explosion. Christian never discussed with me how, or why, this happened. The building was sold, and the Vinassacs' marriage dissolved. My friendship continued with Christian. He would come to my home again for a party, and I heard that he was doing some cooking for private parties and small dinners. A few years would pass and I lost track of him, but I would have liked to continue that friendship.

DANISH FOOD CENTRE

The Danish Food Centre was opened in 1971 and was located at 101 Bloor Street West. It was opened by Danish dairy farmers and operated by the Danish Cheese Association. As a matter of fact, they served over fifty assorted Danish cheeses. The chef was Tommy Abrahamsen, and the staff was trained in Denmark. The female servers were dressed in blue and white and gave a very sanitary and squeaky clean look to the place. It was authentic Danish cuisine, served twice a day. Again, this was a favourite place of mine where you could go and have a quick, superior lunch. This was a very popular lunch destination. The Centre did a lot of catering out. We had a party one evening at my home and I ordered twenty five different kinds of open-faced sandwiches times four, for a total of one hundred sandwiches—what a showpiece of elegance! I don't think the bill came to $300. At today's prices you would pay well over $1000.

They offered a selection of sixty different open-faced Danish sandwiches, a real "smørrebrød," and they always had rare roast beef. They had a wide selection of smoked and fresh fish like salmon, plaice, sole, trout and turbot. These "Gravad Laks" (marinated salmon) with mustard sauce, were a specialty of the house. Upstairs it was more like a cafeteria, but in the Copenhagen Room downstairs they had a hot and cold Scandinavian buffet. Their pastries were the best, less sweet than German and Austrian. Some of the delicious and unique desserts served were "Islagkage Hamlet," a homemade ice cream cake, "Pandekager Hans Christian Andersen," pancakes with a strawberry jam and sugar, and "Wienerbrod Og Kager," Danish pastries. They served the best coffee in town. One of their specialties was a real gem; pork tenderloin stuffed with prunes and apples accompanied by a smooth Danish cold beer or Akvavit—you were in gastronomic paradise.

The Danish Food Centre also sold products like furniture and China made in Denmark. That was the place where my family started the Royal Copenhagen Christmas Plate Collection. At one time we had collected over thirty of them.

FINGERS

Fingers is where I first met Fern Poudrette, who was the chef and a student of Dante Rota. Fern met his beautiful wife, who also worked at Fingers, and they married. She was a very accomplished pianist, but died suddenly. It was a tragedy which changed Fern's life forever. I could feel, and see it, through the years I dealt with him.

Fingers was opened as more of a sideline investment by the owner of Prefab Homes and Cottages, called Viceroy Homes. Fern became a very valued friend of mine, and later I followed him to the other restaurants where he served as chef. Fingers had more of a nightclub atmosphere in its subdued lighting and elegance. It was located at 1240 Bay Street, although the entrance was on Cumberland Avenue near Bellair in the Yorkville Area. The restaurant was originally to be a "finger food" nightclub venture, but did not turn out that way. Fern made excellent use of the large facilities and used the multiple levels to create a very sexy and intimate atmosphere. The food he created accompanied this intimate ambiance. Couples would make an evening of Fingers, starting with cocktails, have a romantic dinner, and then spending the rest of the evening at the disco. Lots of green plants and Tiffany lamps made the place quite comfortable and sensuous. There was an ample selection of meat and seafood, and it was quite affordable. The meat items were of only the highest quality, as I am sure all the other foods were as well. Again, I enjoyed supplying the beef, as there was a plentiful selection of steak on the menu. Fifty dollars, including a tip, would cover dinner and a reasonable wine for two.

THE HOT STOVE

AND MY GOOD FRIEND AND MENTOR— HAROLD BALLARD

I must have driven by the Maple Leaf Gardens and the Hot Stove Lounge hundreds of times in the early 1970s. One day I decided to go in and see if I could sell them something. I knew that on hockey nights they would go through a lot of roast beef and steaks, so I would be the perfect guy to sell them their meat. I walked into the Hot Stove in the morning and was met by a gruff, but amiable, and very approachable, portly man. He asked me what business I had being there and I told him my short story about being in the meat business and wondered if I could be of service to the Hot Stove Lounge. He smiled and invited me to have a coffee while he called the chef, Chris, to come over and talk to me. I guess I was at the right place at the right time. He said that I should not waste too much time talking to him, as lunch was approaching and Chris would be very busy. Chris did speak to me; he asked me to come back again with samples and prices. I returned a few days later and, low and behold, I

Harold Ballard with Miss Tiger Cat and Miss Blue Bomber at Hot Stove Lounge (ca. 1960s)

started to do business with them. The man I had met was Harold E. Ballard, who later became a good friend and mentor.

Going back a few years, the Hot Stove Club Lounge was opened in 1963, but went through some turbulent years. Mr. Paul McNamara, who was the Chariman of the Board at Maple Leaf Gardens, also owned a restaurant complex called Ports of Call. Mr. McNamara's Ports of Call took over management of the Hot Stove. The area around Maple Leaf Gardens was deemed a "dry area" for liquor until the late 1960s. Only wine and beer could be sold. Le Baron, Carman's and Harry's, were all under the same umbrella. This seriously affected the Hot Stove. The Ports of Call experiment did not work out. Enter the Westbury Hotel, which tried to manage the Hot Stove from 1968 to 1971. But that plan did not work either. Finally, Bill Cluff was given the job of general manager of the Hot Stove. It turns out that he was the solution, because Bill turned the Hot Stove into a profitable club, and grew it to become very prosperous.

I sold to the Hot Stove for a few years and then I decided to move to Florida with my family. Things did not work out well in Florida for us, and my wife and I divorced. The good part was that I got custody of my two children, Robin and Tim, and returned to Toronto to start over again. This time, upon returning, I had a good friend waiting for me, Harold Ballard. He welcomed me back and treated me like his son. We started having Friday morning breakfasts on a regular basis, and he took me into his confidence. King Clancy would join us frequently and I loved the spirited and boisterous interaction between them. As a matter of fact, I looked forward to it and it became part of my weekly visit on Friday mornings. It became part of my routine to come to the Hot Stove at least three times a week. The chef let me use his office for any business dealings I had. When I spoke with Harold, mostly one-on-one, he was very genuine and always asked me about my family; he made it possible for me to meet many important people with whom he was associated.

I got to meet people like John D'Amico, Mike Nykoluk, Russ Courtnall, Alan Lamport, Bill Cluff, Nick Loisou, Mary and Bill Ballard, Frank Bonello, Jim Gregory, Mr. Hugh Bruce and a lot of Maple Leaf Gardens staff. Manager of concessions and Harold's chauffeur, Bernie Fournier, and I compared notes weekly. We could have written a book that would have blown out all the doors and windows at the Gardens! During those heydays, rumours and stories were spreading like wild fire and it was great to be a part of it. Harold would tell me things that were very confidential about the organization, and I never revealed them to anyone because of the trust and confidence he had in me. It was always weird to know something was going to happen before it was announced.

Hot Stove Lounge guest register featuring several celebrities, including Muhammad Ali and figure skater Donald Jackson (ca. 1966)

I have read the books written about Harold, and I choose not to comment. As I said, he was a very kind and genuine person to me. He did change when another person or group of individuals came into our space. That was his nature. He was a "carny" who loved to be on. His close newspaper friends were George Gross of the *Telegram* and later *The Sun*, Milt Dunnell of the *Toronto Star* and Dick Beddoes of the *Globe and Mail*. Of course, he would give them the "scoops" first, so it wasn't such a mystery that all of the other media would say he did not treat them fairly. He loved to pick a fight and push the envelope to the point where his adversary got pissed off with him. But I honestly believe that he was still a lover and not a fighter.

John D'Amico and I became close friends up until the time he passed away. There were many times in the winter, although it was very cold and he should not have been out of the house, that he would come to my plant and we would just sit and talk about stuff. He would buy meat and meet with my staff, who had gotten to know him through his visits and seeing him on TV. John really respected and liked Harold and once told me that if there was anything he needed he just had to ask. He complained to Harold about those dumpy dressing rooms that the officials had to use in the old Gardens. Harold listened and had them refurbished. Sadly John died of cancer far too young. I lost a great friend.

Mike Nykoluk became a friend who loved to eat Harold's favourite summer sausage. Chris, the chef, would always order two or three of them for the boss and Mike would come to my plant and buy a few each month. Our friendship developed to the point where, one day, Mike came to my office and asked if I could loan him a few hundred dollars. I knew he was going to "the track" and I did not feel good about it. He asked me if he could leave one of his Stanley Cup rings with me as collateral and for safe keeping. He had been the assistant coach with the Philadelphia Flyers under Fred Shero when they had won two Stanley Cups. I did not know why I refused, but if I had to do it all over again, I would not give it a second thought. One day he said he and his wife were going to move back to the United States and I never heard from him again.

Stan Obodiac, the Maple Leafs' publicist, and a good Ukrainian from Saskatchewan, and I had a special thing going. Anytime he needed an extra pair of hockey tickets he would ask and I would give. And any time I needed an extra pair he was always there. Stan worked diligently up until the day he

died. I saw him a few days before he passed away. He was a real warrior and bled blue and white.

Alan Lamport and I became friends when he became the honorary lifelong General Manager of the Hot Stove Lounge. I remember when he received the Order of Canada on October 19, 1994. Obviously he was so proud. He sent me a copy of the cover and first page of the citation as read in Rideau Hall at the investiture of the Order of Canada as Governor General Ray Hnatyshyn, another good Ukrainian, pinned on "Lampy." He had been in public service for thirty-six years. Mr. Toronto was a member of the Ontario legislature, an alderman, Mayor of the city of Toronto, a controller and the chairman of the Toronto Transit Commission. He was a staunch supporter of subsidized housing, but he is best known for the key role he played in the construction of Canada's first subway system, and in bringing Sunday sports to Toronto. It is him I can thank for going to those Sunday afternoon Marlie and St. Mike's junior "A" games with my father, John. All of those Stanley Cups won by the Toronto Maple Leafs in the '60s were stocked with players from those Marlie and St. Mike's teams. Eddie Shack would come in with the Guelph Biltmores, Bobby Hull and Stan Mikita with the St. Catherine's Tee Pees, and Henry Richard the Pocket Rocket with the Montreal junior Canadiens to name a few. "Lampy" was the last person to visit Harold before he died. I was the second last.

Dick Beddoes, wearing his very fashionable and colourful Homburg hats, sat two rows in front of me at Maple Leaf Gardens in the "golds," on the goal line in the south east corner. I would greet him with "Hi Dickie" and his answer would be "Hi Meatman!" He wrote in his book *Pal Hal*—"to Ron who supplies the best meat in the history of the Hot Stove

Lounge. You have more meat than any Leaf player, except Wendel Clark. When people say mainly because of the meat—they mean YOUR meat."

All of the gold seats had a hat rack under each seat, however, Dick never took his hat off during the game. I have two of those Homburg "chapeaus" and I think of him every time I put one on. He, too, passed away far too early.

Dan Maloney was a rough-tough, two-way, hockey player who could irritate the piss out of any opposing player. My son wore his number nine on his Maple Leaf sweater as long as Danny played for the Leafs. I was watching a practice one morning with Harold when he leaned over and said that Danny would be his next coach. Low and behold, a month later that became the truth. He was a real brawler and could be rated as one of the toughest Leafs.

Russ Courtnall was a rookie from Langley, BC who I saw progress with the Maple Leafs. He was probably the most graceful skater next to Dave Keon. We became friends and visited each other's homes for barbeques, and I would have liked to have had him as my son if I could. Trading him to Montreal for John Kordic was probably one of the stupidest trades of all time.

Alan Eagleson's office would call me once a month and order 12 to 20 boxes of the finest assorted US choice steaks. His office became as good a customer as some of my regular restaurant customers. I got paid as soon as the meat was delivered, so I considered him an AAA customer.

Bill Cluff became a good friend. He was the General Manager of the Hot Stove Lounge, and I dealt with him on a regular basis. His sister Pat became the wife of Herbert Gregory, a securities analyst who I worked with at Bache and Company in the late '60s. Bill was very professional and organized, initiating much needed sanity at the Hot Stove. Nick Loisou was the manager under Bill, and has helped me research the facts and history of this chapter.

Mary and Bill Ballard became personal friends of mine who I cherish to this day. I was fortunate to meet Mike Flynn, Mary's second husband, who often came by the plant to buy meat from me. He died tragically of a heart attack. Unfortunately, I did not get to meet or know Harold Jr. I know Mary, Bill and Harold persevered through much controversy during the outrageous battles that were blown out of proportion in the press. Although I am well informed about the Ballard wars. My position is not to report what has already been written about—truthfully or not. I have always been treated graciously and respectfully by the Ballards, and can appreciate how they felt and will always feel the way they do. Remember, you can say what you want about Harold Sr., but, in the end, he took care of his family. Bill Ballard unfortunately passed away in March, 2014.

Frank Bonello played hockey and worked in the meat industry for Canada Packers. Frank spent 34 years with Canada Packers from 1955 to 1989, selling to the retail and chain store trade. This is how I first met him through Joe Dermastja. He played center for the Whitby Dunlops, who won the Ontario Seniors championship in 1956, the Allen Cup in 1957, and the World Championship in 1958. He served two years as coach of the Toronto Marlboroughs from 1970 to 1972 and sixteen years as General Manager from 1972 to 1988. He then became Director of Central Scouting for the

National Hockey League for nineteen years, from 1989 to 2008. Harold usually had the last word in any decisions made regarding the Marlboroughs, but he had so much respect and trust for Frank that he left all the decisions to him. He truly was one of Harold's closest employees. Frank was also a personal retail customer of mine and we would share many stories when we met. One day he brought Jim Gregory to my place and another friendship started. Both bought great steaks for their families and cottage.

Jim Gregory served as General Manager of the Toronto Maple Leafs Hockey Organization for ten years, from 1969 to 1979. He was also the president of the Toronto affiliates in Tulsa and Phoenix. When he was let go in 1979, he immediately became the Vice President of Hockey Operations for the National Hockey League. During his tenure with the Leafs, he drafted Darryl Sittler and Errol Thompson in 1970, Lanny McDonald in 1973, and Randy Carlyle in 1976. He also signed Borje Salmong and Inge Hammerstrom from Sweden. Here is a cute story Jim told me once: The Leafs had an affiliation with the Hershey Bears hockey team in Hershey, Pennsylvania. Frank Mathers was a defenceman with the Leafs and later became a player and coach with the Hershey Bears. Obviously there was a connection between chocolate and the city of Hershey, and every time Frank Mathers came to Toronto he would bring Jim some chocolate. This continued until, one day, Jim noticed that he was not getting those chocolate gifts anymore. Now, it was no secret that Harold had a very big sweet tooth. Jim asked his secretaries why Frank did not bring any chocolates to his office. Well, you can guess what was happening. Someone was taking those treats out of Jim's office. Guess who? Harold,

a diabetic, should not have been eating chocolate. For special holidays like Christmas and Easter I would provide chocolate mousse baskets, which I fully believed were going to his family as gifts. Later I found out that he was eating them. Here I was feeding the man poison!

Hugh Bruce also became a good friend. I had originally met Mr. Bruce through my good friend and lawyer, Norman Tomas. Norman articled with the law firm of Bruce Delzotto and Zorzi in the early '60s. I met Mr. Bruce at Norman's house on many occasions. I met him again at the Hot Stove Lounge where he was a senior advisor and long standing member. He and Mr. Lamport were very dear friends, and he became a good customer of mine for many years.

Harold Ballard always put his money where his mouth was. That proved true when he bought the Hamilton Tiger Cats in 1978. The Cats won the eastern championship four times and the Grey Cup in 1986. He sold the Tiger Cats in 1988. He had saved them, but had lost over $20 million. So I had to wear a blue and white Maple Leaf jacket that was also coloured yellow and gold with a tiger cat on one half.

The new Hot Stove in the Air Canada Centre is not the same bygone club from the Gardens. I understand the old Hot Stove was sort of an afterthought when everything moved to the Air Canada Centre. However, the new version seats one hundred and sixty guests for dining and has about forty seats at the bar, but the larger space at the ACC means there are many more facilities to provide drink and food options. Without everyone packing into one spot, that passionate and avid atmosphere that inhabited the old Hot Stove will never be duplicated.

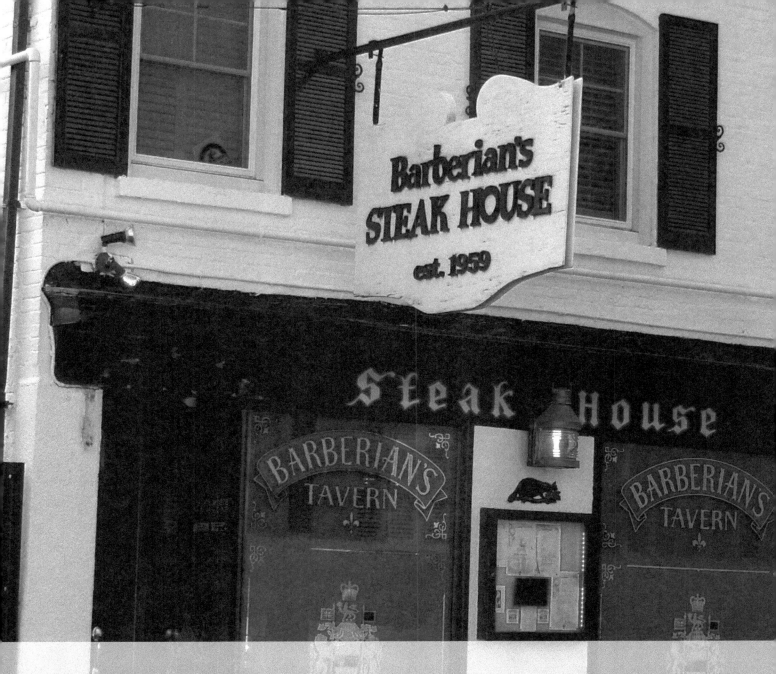

BARBERIAN'S
STEAK HOUSE

Harry Barberian (ca. 1970s)

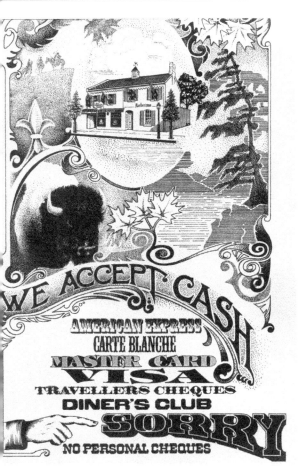

You could probably write a complete book on Harry Barberian and his life in the restaurant business. I hope that will someday come to pass. I must say, Harry became a good friend of mine in the late '60s up until he died on October 28, 2001. Anybody in the restaurant business from the '50s all the way through to the '90s knew Harry Barberian. To those who didn't, I will try to fill in some facts.

Harry quit school in his hometown of Brantford, Ontario in grade eight, and spent the next ten years working in a farm machinery assembly plant until was laid off. He then took a job in a greasy spoon while working at a Wasaga Beach hot dog stand, and in 1955 accepted a job at Le Baron. Harry also gave up a promising career in professional theatre. He was a student with Amelia Piscatore's world famous drama workshop in New York, which had students such as Anthony Perkins, Marilyn Monroe and Marlon Brando. However, the CBC did not offer Harry any opportunities when he returned to Canada, so it was back to his calling—the restaurant business.

Barberian's opened in 1959 when steakhouses were just starting to open. A very small, quaint, cottage-style building with a hearth on Elm Street became available and Harry bought it. Initially it held about 26 people. He added 22 seats after the bordello next door was closed. The building was built in 1860 and, to this day, maintains the charm of a structure built way back then. He was known as the 'Toots Shor of Toronto' after the famed New York restaurateur and barkeep who was a confidante to numerous celebrities. Elizabeth Taylor and Richard Burton announced their first engagement here in 1964. The Soviet Army Chorus invaded the restaurant when they were in Toronto and singing and dancing prevailed all night long. Rudolph Nureyev, Robert Morley, Sir Ralph Richardson and Sir John Gielgud became returning guests. Harry's trademark was buying a Rolls Royce and chauffeuring customers to and from Harry's and Barberian's when he needed to—a certain steakhouse still does that now and it certainly is a great calling card.

Harry was introduced to cooking by his mother, who was introduced to cooking by Auguste Escoffier in England. So it is no wonder that Harry was so connected to the Escoffier Society in Toronto. We would go to the monthly meetings on the first Monday of every month, and it became habit for me to meet Harry and sit with him and discuss all the latest goings-on in the restaurant and meat business. We would always exchange small gifts at these meetings. I became a member of the ancient order of Chaine Des Rôtisseurs, and Harry's medal is still on display in the restaurant when you enter. Harry achieved the honour of Maître Rôtisseur.

Harry was a great storyteller. He could tell you thousands of stories if time permitted, and I learned so much from him. I grew to be "wild about Harry." The Canadian Broadcasting Company (CBC) was located behind the Le Baron restaurant on Jarvis Street and performers and staff would come by Le Baron after work was done. Harry would be outside in the back for a breath of fresh air and a smoke, and would indulge in conversation with these people. When Harry decided to go into his own endeavor, these people followed him. As mentioned, I got to know Harry in the late '60s. His meat supplier was Benny Winbaum, who owned Vaunclair Purveyors and a company called Winco, with various locations that primarily served steak. Harry always bought the highest US choice and US prime beef when available and had his own aging program. His son, Arron, carries on the program to this day along with Jose Iribarren, Scott Thompson and Bob Berman.

During my time with Honeyman Beef Purveyors, I started to get to know the chef at Berberian's, Gerhard Neubauer. He had been trained to be a Konditorei-Chocolatiere, but was also trained as a very proficient pastry chef and received his full chef's papers. He mastered the charcoal grill and helped Barberian's become a dining institution, and they still use wood charcoal to this day. I would go into the restaurant on Sunday evenings after dinner to visit Gerhard and get the main meat order for the week. After a while, my wife would ask me where I was going on a Sunday night after 9:00 pm. I'm sure she did not believe me when I said that I was going to see a customer. I remember Gerhard's apple beignets, which became legendary. He would always add a touch of Cognac or Armenac. No Sunday night would pass without my having that treat. I would always call on Thursdays for Friday delivery to keep supplies stocked, and Gerhard and I developed a close relationship. This relationship extended to our families, as I have watched the two Neubauer boys, Alexander and Oliver, grow into fine young adults.

In 1976, Harry sold his business (a twenty year deal) to Weir Ross and Rob Hansen. Gerhard stayed on for a while and business carried on while Steve Rigakos stayed on and became chef. They enjoyed continued success, but, although I enjoyed being their meat supplier, it was never quite the same. After he sold his business, Harry would travel to and from Palm Beach in Florida where he and his family had a home. He had contacted and spent his time as a consultant to the restaurant business in Canada and the United States. I was also living in Florida in the late '70s and I will always remember the story that Harry told me: "Ronnie, if I were ever to open another restaurant, I would open a breakfast-only place. I would open from 6:00 am to 3:00 pm daily, and close on Sundays. I would serve 3 eggs, 3 strips of bacon, home fries, toast and coffee for $3.00 and I know it would be an instant success." He had a friend in Florida who owned a business just as Harry described that put both his kids through medical and law school in the finest and most expensive universities in the country. The owner became very wealthy. Harry told me that he sold 500 to 600 breakfasts a day.

In 1994 Harry took his business back, and Barberian's continued to rate as one of the best steak houses in the city. His son Arron, and his ever wonderful and faithful wife Helen, helped carry on the tradition. Harry and Helen had another son, Michael, who decided that the restaurant business was not for him and stayed in the United States; I believe he continues to live there, working as a master woodworker. If Harry was still alive, how proud he would be to see his son Arron carrying on the family tradition. He is involved in many projects and charities and has helped me with this chapter. It is incredible that he is so well informed and up to date on past and present hospitality details. He has added much new Canadiana to the Vintage collection that was already there, as Harry had a wonderful art collection, including a number of works by the Group of Seven (he was a good friend of A.J. Casson).

I remember when Harry turned sixty. He had a birthday brunch party at the Delta Chelsea that my wife Florence and I had been invited to, along with his family and close friends. As I looked around the crowd I did not recognize any other suppliers. One day I invited Harry and Helen up to my home in Erin for a barbeque. But Helen did not feel well that day so instead he brought up a friend named Domenic Zoffranieri, who was the executive chef of the Chelsea Inn and served as President of the Escoffier Society in Toronto. They barbequed the steaks, showing me how humble they could be. I was truly blessed that Harry had thought of me as a friend as well as a trusted supplier.

Many of the owners and waiters that I still talk to remember Harry Barberian, and many worked for him. No one has ever had a bad word to say about him. Harry had a saying: 'If you don't like the steak, don't pay for it' and that was a motto that I adopted in my business: 'If you don't like the meat, you don't have to pay for it.' He planted many seeds in the industry he loved so much. He helped Ed Mirvish start his own beef emporium. He owned a place called Harry's on Church Street, just north of Le Baron, where he and George Bigliardi started, before he opened his own place on Church Street. Tom Jones Steak House sprouted from a Harry Barberian seed. Harry probably left his fingerprints on every steakhouse in Toronto and I would rate Barberian's as one of the best establishments in North America.

MEMORABLE STEAK EXPERIENCES

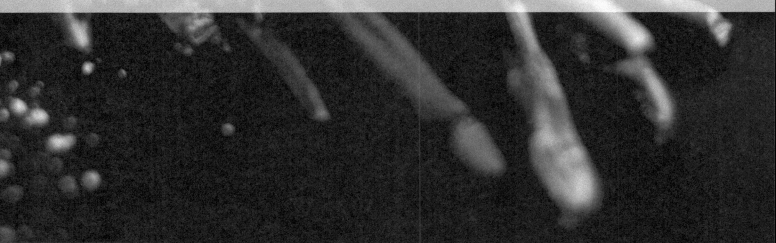

LE BARON STEAK HOUSE

Le Baron opened at 425 Church Street in 1955. Frank Kiss, the owner, hired Harry Barberian as his chef and thus Harry's life began in the Toronto steakhouse business. Le Baron was actually the second steakhouse opened in Toronto after the Sign of the Steer. In a very short time Le Baron became very successful, with the Maple Leaf Gardens providing a steady stream of steak-loving customers. Steaks were featured in a glass case where customers could choose which they wanted to be grilled. Waiters wore red jackets in a restaurant that was brown and white with lots of wood and brick; a Medieval wall mural by Van Svoboda of horses, dogs and men in armour adorned one of the main walls. During these early times, a 16 oz. bone-in rib steak would sell for $2.25, a 16 oz. New York sirloin for $2.50 and tenderloin was not featured. A fresh shrimp cocktail sold for 75 cents.

A second Le Baron Steak House (II) was opened later at 663 Yonge Street at Charles, but it never enjoyed the patronage that the original did.

BARDI'S

Bardi's has always been one of the better steakhouses in Toronto. Located at 56 York Street across from the Royal York Hotel, Bardi's is a restaurant that I have never sold one ounce of any kind of meat to. Phil Bardwell started Bardi's, but did not last long in the tough business and went into receivership. Alex Manikas, took over the business and made it a success. Manikas was always very respectful to me, as I was to him. We met on different occasions at meat conferences, and I know he always bought the very best quality product available. He would not have been in the business for long if that were not true. Bardi's has always specialized in steak, and did not initially focus on items like escargot and seafood. From its early days, because Bardi's was located across from the Royal York Hotel, many visiting athletes and entertainers would come to drink and dine as they do to this day. I'm sure that Bardi's can safely boast that they have entertained their fair share of sports celebrities in Toronto.

ZORRO'S

Zorro's opened in September of 1975 at 7171 Torbram Road in Mississauga. On opening day, September 18, only two people showed up. But never again! The word spread quickly and Zorro's became an instant classic. Nick Iatropoulos and Frank Athanasiou became owners of this fabulous steakhouse. It was located minutes from the Pearson International Airport, airport hotels and the International Centre. Nick got his earlier dining training at Hy's and La Castile; Frank also served his time at La Castile. This restaurant always bought the finest, top quality U.S. Choice and U.S Prime beef, and the best premium seafood. They were voted to have the best Prime Rib over the years. Frank was bought out by Nick in May of 2008 and Zorro's is now managed by Nick and his two son-in-laws, John and Menno. They continue to carry on the superior tradition of Zorro's.

HY'S

Hy's originally opened at 73 Richmond St. West and became the home of the big steak and served superb drinks that were probably the best cocktails in the city. Hy Aisenstat founded the Hy's chain in 1955. A lot of my lawyer friends swore that Hy's had the best drinks, and so it became a second home for them. They developed a large lunch crowd from the legal and business community. It became like a private club with a comfortable ambiance.

I was quite fortunate and pleased to become a supplier to Hy's and had the good fortune to meet Gary Griffin, who became the chef there and later a friend and friendly competitor. Hy's has always used high-quality Canadian beef for their restaurants. Hy's bought tenderloins, striploins and top butts from me. In 1971, a 16 oz. tenderloin was $9.00 and an 8 oz. New York sirloin was $6.00. What a great time to eat red meat! A second Hy's was opened at 133 Yorkville and seemed more luxurious, but was never as popular as the original. Hy's opened a sister operation called "Sherlocks" at 12 Sheppard, behind and down the street from 73 Richmond Street, which was a specialty roast beef restaurant. As time passed the three locations closed, but Hy's opened a new place on Adelaide Street which is still very popular.

HARBOUR SIXTY STEAKHOUSE

Harbour Sixty was opened in 1999 by Ted Nikolaou. Originally immigrating from Greece at the young age of thirteen, Ted opened his first restaurant at twenty-two in new Toronto called the Rex Grill; next came a chain of restaurants called JJ Muggs located in Toronto and vicinity. That was the initial contact I had with them. They catered to the private boxes at Maple Leaf Gardens and they serviced private boxes at the Air Canada Centre and restaurant.

Ted opened Harbour Sixty in the impressive Toronto Harbour Commission building at 60 Harbour Street. Previously the building had accommodated a very lovely restaurant in the 1970s and 1980s, which had been a customer of mine. Now, as the neighbourhood changed, Harbour Sixty is located in the most busy cosmopolitan area of Toronto. It sits across the street from the Air Canada Centre. It is very cool and fashionable, and the ambiance is very glamorous and comfortable. It is the place to be seen.

The restaurant serves superb quality US prime beef, US choice lamb and milk fed veal. The seafood matches the quality of their red meat and other protein. Ted was the first to use bone-in tenderloin steaks, as well as the tomahawk, a French bone-in rib steak weighing in at 40 to 45 oz. The restaurant has an open kitchen so that patrons can see and choose what they want to eat.

They also have a huge catering arm called Pinnacle Catering, and cater to private and corporate barbeques. Ted was a close friend to the late Steve Stavro who owned the Toronto Maple Leafs and the Maple Leaf Gardens. Ted , his son Steve, daughter Lisa and some very capable people run the Harbour Sixty on a daily basis. On any given Maple Leafs hockey night Ted can also be seen behind the Toronto Maple Leaf hockey teams bench in the first row with his buddy Ken Stathakis of the Octagon.

HARRY'S
STEAK HOUSE

Harry's was located at 518 Church Street, two blocks north of Maple Leaf Gardens, and was formerly owned by my good friend Harry Barberian. It used to be known as Romanelli's, but opened as Harry's in 1960. The menus were the same at both Harry's and his other restaurant, Barberian's. They only had five meat items; four were steaks and the other was shish kebab of lamb. This was Harry's specialty and was served with kalamata olives and feta cheese.

At one time Harry owned Barberian's and Harry's and decided to sell Harry's in December 1966 to the Martin brothers from Paris, Ontario. They were involved in the lithography business known as the Walker Press Limited. They had offices in Toronto and New York. They also owned Kaumagraph and had a successful horse breeding farm providing contenders for the Queen's Plate and other major stake races. Jack and Verne Martin bought Harry's and immediately hired George Bigliardi to manage it. George was the head waiter at the Oak Room of the King Edward Hotel in Toronto. I met George at Harry's and became a supplier to his restaurant. Ten years later, in 1976, George bought a restaurant across the street and established a great steakhouse in the '80s. To this day, I am a friend to Chris Tripodi, daughter of Jack Martin and her husband Tony. Both Chris and her husband Tony have been private loyal meat customers of mine. Harry's is no longer, and the location has passed into different hands.

Harry's Steak House, exterior (1971)

I Don't turn my Keys over to just ANYONE!!

I am most pleased to announce that HARRY'S has been purchased by my two very good friends, Mr. Verne and Jack Martin of Paris Ont.

I know that you will find them to be excellent Hosts, and always considerate of your pleasure and comfort.

I wish them every success in this new venture.

We're looking Forward to greeting you at HARRY'S and to continuing the Tradition of the BEST STEAKS IN TOWN.

Martin Brothers

Jack   Verne

HARRY'S, 518 Church St.

Paris Star Dec 8, 1966

EL TORO STEAKHOUSE

El Toro was opened at 39 Colborne Street behind the King Edward Hotel. It was probably my earliest favourite steakhouse only because my office at Bache and Company was at 18 King St. East. I was not in the meat business yet. When I had a really great day, I would always treat myself to a large bone-in rib steak. This was also garlic heaven, where you could indulge in a loaf of some of the best garlic bread in Toronto. In the summer, it was very "bistro-ish" and the windows would open completely and air conditioning was not a problem. I felt like I was eating in Mexico or some Spanish hacienda. Time passed and this restaurant closed.

SIGN OF THE STEER

The Sign of the Steer was actually the first steak house opened in Toronto by Hans Fread at the junction of Davenport and Dupont. I did not have the pleasure of supplying this restaurant because it opened in 1950 and I was only nine years old. I cannot comment much about the Sign of the Steer because there was not too much information to be found, and it did not last long before steak places like Le Baron, Carman's and Barberian's took the spotlight. Moreover, the Sign of the Steer steaks were not charcoal broiled, but pan fried; no comparison to the newly opening steakhouses that were emerging.

Peppio's restaurant and tavern, an Italian flavoured restaurant, followed the Sign of the Steer. Peppio's was where Ken Stathakis started. Ken and his son, Steve, run the present day Octagon Steakhouse in Thornhill.

Sign of Steer, exterior (1955)

GEORGE BIGLIARDI'S STEAK HOUSE

George Bigliardi opened his namesake establishment in 1977. The majority of his customers followed him across the street from Harry's and, as mentioned, Bigliardi's became a great steak house. George attracted many celebrities with his outgoing personality, and was known to practice in and enjoy the sport of kings, horse racing. He served fabulous steaks to his loyal customers and became a legend. Bigliardi's became the most popular steak house of the Toronto Maple Leaf hockey players and their families. Steak lovers and good friends John and Mary Newediuk, founders of the Newediuk Funeral Homes, ate there before attending Leafs games faithfully over many years. Frank Sinatra, Bette Midler and even Pope John Paul II visited Bigliardi's. We, as a company, were proud to count Bigliardi's as one of our valued customers. One fact that was not publicized was that George Bigliardi had first dibs on the Harbour Sixty location, but turned it down. He had had his glory and I guess it was time to give someone else their chance at success. Harbour Sixty Steakhouse took that opportunity and turned it into the tremendous steak house operation it is today. Again, I was very proud to be a part of their success.

TOM JONES STEAK HOUSE

Again, Harry Barberian weaves his magic. Harry took a lease on a building at 17 Leader Lane which became Tom Jones Steak House in 1966. One of his managers, George Goutzioulis, was the benefactor when he bought it in 1976. George was a soft spoken and very personable gentleman, and created and served very delicious prime steaks and seafood selections. The restaurant was located in the heart of the financial and theatre districts, next to the King Edward Hotel. This building was constructed in the early 1830s in "Olde York Towne," and is truly a historic landmark with open flame, gaslight chandeliers. Because of the unique design of the building and its private areas, corporate luncheons and dinners, before and after theatre dinner parties, could easily be arranged. Cocktail parties for up to 150, buffets from 80 to 100, special anniversaries, retirements, wedding receptions and Christmas parties all were easily accommodated, along with special menus for all occasions. George has always been a truly congenial host.

Tom Jones
Steakhouse & Seafood
Circa 1966

17 Leader Lane, Toronto, Ontario
Tel: (416) 366-6583-4
Fax: (416) 366-7233

In the heart of the Financial and Theatre District
next to The King Edward Hotel

Menu Highlights

Fresh Gulf Shrimp Cocktail
Fresh Smoked Scottish Salmon
Escargots "Bourguignonne"
New England Clam Chowder
Caesar Salad

Prime Rib Roast of Beef with Rosemary Au Jus
Filet Mignon wrapped with Bacon
Prime New York Striploin
Grilled Breast of Free Range Chicken
Provimi Veal Chops with Port Wine Sauce
Provimi Rack of Lamb "for two"
Chateaubriand "for two"

Lobster Tail and Filet Mignon
Broiled Scampi
Dover Sole "Almandine"
Filet of Fresh Red Snapper
Live Lobster

The Best Prime Beef Available

Weekday Hours
Monday to Friday 11:30 am – 1:30 am

CARMAN'S

Carman's Restaurant, exterior (1973)

The third steak house to open in Toronto was Carman's in 1959. It was located at 26 Alexander Street, just up the street from Maple Leaf Gardens. You could smell the garlic a block away. Arthur Carman (born Athanasios Karamanos), a young chef who came to Canada from Greece in the early '50s, cooked in Montreal and Toronto and ultimately joined with partners and created his own steakhouse. From the beginning, Arthur Carman used Canadian beef and dealt with Canada Packers and then Honeyman Beef Purveyors. It was not until the late 1990s that he converted to US choice product and J.J. Derma Meats became his supplier. He was one of the first people to use portion control, which meant that his steaks were pre-cut to a specified size. That way he had more control over what a steak would cost him. He had no waste factor and could control his inventory as well. He had his waiters carry small flashlights to make sure the steaks were done correctly for his patrons.

Arthur was a very determined person, so his was probably one of the hardest restaurants to convert as a supplier. Arthur maintained that he was the first to use garlic on his steaks at Carman's, but I'm sure others would not agree. Some would say he used garlic to an excess, but it became very popular. Mr. Carman claimed that he had a hand in starting the tradition of the "caravan," an annual celebration of ethnic nationalities in Toronto where each country's food was featured at different locations. I believe that Mr. Leon Kossar also had a hand in originating the "caravan" tradition. This was disputed by many, but every time I dined with Arthur, he claimed that he was right and everyone else was wrong. I would never spend less than four hours at Carman's when I visited for dinner. I could never win a debate with Arthur. In the end, he imagined a lot of things, mistrusted people and suffered dementia. He met, hosted and entertained many people. He truly was a celebrity and a remarkable person.

HOUSE OF CHAN

The "Chan" was opened in 1958 by Irv Howard, a pharmacist and former truck dealer, at 876 Eglinton Ave West, near Bathurst. This was the first steakhouse in Toronto to use US prime beef, although I do know Sam Shopsowitz used US prime beef briskets at his Shopsy's delicatessen. East coast lobster was also served here. No reservations were ever taken. Irv owned this place for twenty years, but sold to Donald (Doc) Lyons in 1978. Doc offered shares of ownership to a very select few regular patrons of the "Chan." By 1992, Doc bought out all shares except one. This remarkable hang out for Forest Hill Jews and Rosedale 'WASPs' boasted long lines of Rolls Royces, Bentleys and Mercedes-Benzes along Eglinton in parking, and no parking, lanes. This establishment has not changed for over 50 years and is in a time warp. Decorated with lanterns and lots of red, this restaurant resembled a classic 1950s-era Chinese restaurant. It is expected to be demolished to make way for a new TTC transit station in 2014. In 2009, Doc Lyons died and left his wife Penny in charge. I did most of my dealings with Rigby Kwok and I regret that I did not participate more in dealing with the House of Chan.

THE OCTAGON

I would safely say that the Octagon Steak House is a landmark in Thornhill and Toronto. Ken Stathakis opened the Octagon in 1973 at 7529 Yonge Street where the Copper Kettle once stood. Ken started at Peppio's, a popular Italian restaurant where the Sign of the Steer once was, and moved over to Harry's on Church Street. George Bigliardi, as mentioned, had a hand in the early beginnings of many restaurateurs. Ken and his son, Steve, developed the Octagon into one of the premier steakhouses in Toronto. They upgraded their red meat to US prime quality and it is second to none. With their fussy but discriminating clientele, they set the steakhouse bar at the highest level. The artistic stained glass, brass lighting fixtures, rich wood and finely upholstered furniture all made for a warm and relaxing ambiance. I have known some of their very experienced wait staff and kitchen personnel for years. On any given night that the Toronto Maple Leafs play at the Air Canada Centre you may see Ken or Steve sitting directly behind the Leaf's bench. They are truly Maple Leaf fans.

THE CATTLE BARON STEAKHOUSE AND TAVERN

The Cattle Baron was opened in 1973 by John Skandalakis in Waterdown, Ontario. This truly was a West End steakhouse, located at Clappisons Corners at the corners of Highway 5 and 6. The restaurant was on the north-east corner. John also owned the north-west corner and the south-east corner. He could have had the south-west corner, but a large oil and gas company would not sell. The Cattle Baron was certainly a destination in the nub of nowhere. The restaurant had a very inviting and comfortable dining room with accommodations for small and large banquets. Soup and a sandwich were always waiting for me when I came to take my order for the week. I will never forget that. Quality was never an issue, because John used the best and the place was always busy. Weddings and special occasions were welcome, because ample parking was always available. John and his wife Irene treated me very well and I am now also good friends with their son George. Regrettably the Cattle Baron has been closed for some years.

THE BLACK ANGUS STEAK HOUSE

Black Angus, exterior (ca. 1990)

The Black Angus was opened on November 28, 1964 and was originated by the Jako family. The steakhouse has stayed in the Toronto West and Kingsway communities. Many restaurants have come and gone throughout the last 50 years, but the Black Angus has survived because of the consistent high quality US choice beef products that they serve. The Black Angus became loyal customers of J.J. Derma Meats in the early '80s and continued for 30 years. Their specialty of the house, which was originally a 20 oz. bone-in rib steak and which has now been increased to 22 oz., is my favourite.

Many private retail customers were referred to J.J. Derma Meats in those years and have become trusted and loyal friends. The restaurant was sold in 2013 and was completely and tastefully renovated, still serving a great steak. Harry Cardiakos, the President, has kept most of the original waiters who are there to welcome and cater to their faithful diners. Many of the original patrons have brought their children here and that tradition carries on.

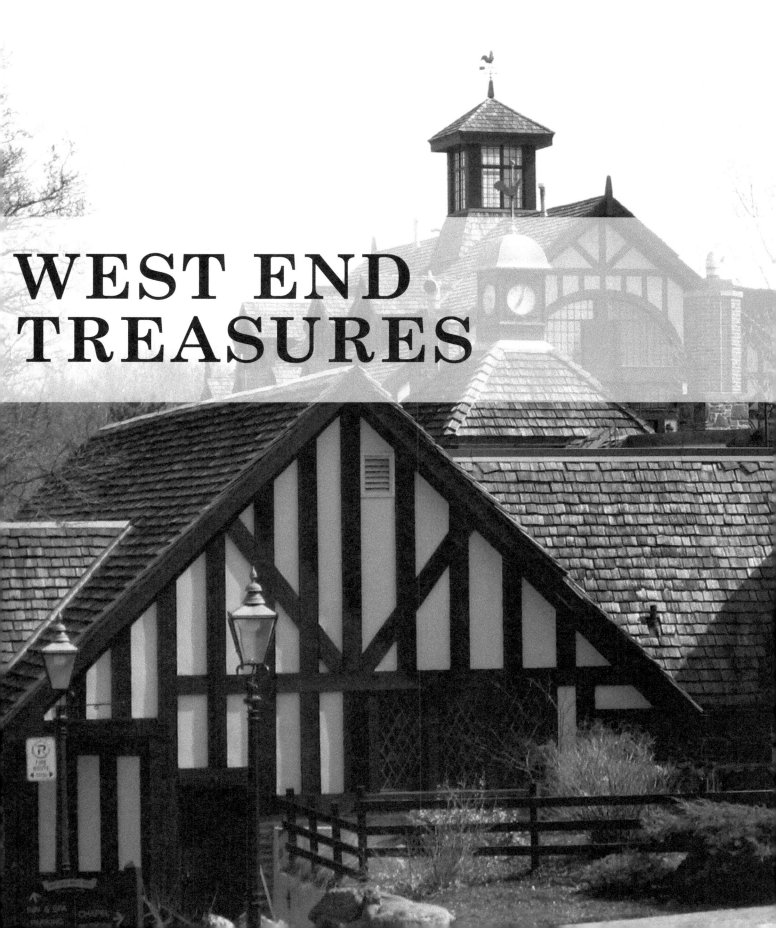

WEST END
TREASURES

ASCOT INN

The Ascot Inn was opened in 1968 in Rexdale at Highway 27 across from the Woodbine Racetrack. The Inn was built and owned by the same owner of the Walker House. This place had a Swiss look to it, dining facilities and 100 rooms. The dining room was called the Iron Kettle and served quite unconventional food, such as buffalo steaks, goose, arctic char and was a take-off on the Walker House. The menu was expensive.

With the close proximity to the airport and the race track, this establishment became very popular in a short period. However, it also gained a notorious reputation as a center for the disposal of stolen cars, and a meeting place for afternoon delights. This was a perfect refuge, not too far from the city, and yet very close to action. Later, Chrysalis bought the Ascot Inn property and it was turned into a nightclub entertainment center.

LATINA TAVERN

The Latina Tavern and Restaurant opened at 690 Queensway in Etobicoke across from the Hollywood Hotel, which is now a Gentleman's club. Latina, deriving its name from a province in Italy, developed a great reputation and was very popular. The owner was Luigi Orgera, and the menu was Northern Italian. Pastas were all fresh and handmade, and the menu was predominantly fish and seafood. The Zabaione Masala sold for a buck. I mention this place because I passed it almost every day. I did not sell them anything, but it is a treasure because it was inexpensive and served top quality products.

THE MUSKET

The Musket opened thirty five years ago, in 1978, by Helmut Enser. This hidden gem, although popular in the Etobicoke area, has gained quite a reputation on the food network as a place to eat. Joanne Enser was also an owner of the Musket with her husband Helmut. The Musket derives its name from Helmut's collection of old musket rifles, and he thought that the name was appropriate. Some of them are on display in the restaurant. Richard Enser, the son of Helmut, is the executive chef and has spared no expense on the quality food that the Musket serves. The steak they serve is as good as any steakhouse. The portions are large so do come hungry! Delightful appetizers, delicious soups and divine salads are a prelude to the main courses. Specialties like three different kinds of schnitzel, smoked pork chops (Kessler), roulade and their specialty the large barbeque pork hocks the size of boxing gloves. There is a meat platter for two patterned after King Henry VIII's ravenous appetite. Sauerkraut or Bavarian red cabbage and home fries accompany most of these dishes. Bockwurst and Brotwurst are both featured on the luncheon menu. Apple strudel, hazelnut, chocolate mousse, sacher or cheese cake are great companions to their continental liquor–inspired coffees. The imported draught beers: Hacker Pschorr Weisse, Edel Hill, Munich Dark to Warsteiner, Krombacher and Furstenberg are from Germany. As of this writing, Helmut passed away and Joanne and his son, Richard, will now manage the restaurant.

Welcome To

THE

MUSKET

Dining Lounge Banquet Facilities

It is our sincere hope that you will thoroughly enjoy your dinner with us today.

Should this be a special occasion, please let us know if there is any way in which we can make this evening a more memorable one for you... ...recommending a fine Wine to go with your selections from our menu... ...or one of our delicious special Continental Coffees to wrap up the night.

Seasoned professionals welcome the opportunity to cater to all your dining needs!

THE DOCTOR'S HOUSE AND LIVERY

The Doctor's House in Kleinberg originally dates back to 1867. It was originally a house owned by Doctor James Stephenson, who sold it to Doctor Thomas Harvey Robinson, who practiced there for 52 years. The Gordon MacEachern family bought the house in 1961 and turned it into a tearoom in 1971. A restaurant was opened to cater to the patrons who visited the McMichael Art Gallery, which displayed the world's largest collection of paintings by the Group of Seven. I was very fortunate to get to know A.J. Casson and enjoyed his works immensely. The Livery was opened in 1974 by John MacEachern, the son, who inherited the business and took it to another level. The restaurant is near the Portage Route travelled by the Indians and early explorers from Lake Ontario to Lake Simcoe along the Credit River. The Livery took on the appearance of a large stable adorned with huge foot-square wooden beams, massive fireplaces, and decorated with Ontario antiques made in the Kleinberg area, as well as Canadiana farming tools. The recipes were inspired by early Canadian cuisine. Some of the house specialties were duck, Ontario pheasant, and saddle or hare interspersed by traditional continental fare. There was a wide choice of steaks, roast beef and seafood items. Many prices were quite reasonable to make up for the trek up to Kleinberg.

Here's a great story for you. John MacEachern himself admitted that he was the owner of a haunted building, the Livery in Kleinberg, but the actual story begins with the tearoom in the early 1960's. There was this old print of Alice in Wonderland that hung on one wall, but every morning it would be on the floor. One day the previous owners, who had lived in the house for ten years, asked Mrs. MacEachern if she had noticed her "friend" around, the ghost. Part of the puzzle seemed to have been solved. Well, in 1974, when the Livery was built, the "ghost" followed. A night cleaner was working one evening after the restaurant was closed. All kinds of commotion and a ruckus could be heard upstairs. Chairs would be piled in the middle of the floor. The cleaner was freaked out and did not return.

The MacEacherns had their own janitorial business, so it was decided that they would do their own cleaning. Strange things like moving candles on tables, candles being relit after they were blown out, doors opening and closing by themselves, and the pages of a guest book turning by themselves, were starting to happen. The lights in the dining room would dim nightly and Vaughan Hydro would have no explanation. The ghost was given the name "Caesar." There was a guest one evening who had no previous knowledge of the antics going on at the restaurant, but he had felt very uneasy all evening and claimed that the place was haunted. Having experiences with physic happenings, he said the ghost was that of an old man with white hair who was half Indian and half Irish. The man was said to have been buried in a graveyard a very short distance away where, unknown to the physic, a graveyard was actually located. These tales have now expired, but it reminds me of the old Abbott and Costello antics in their hilarious old movies.

Your host: John MacEachern

The Doctor's House and Livery is rapidly acquiring an international reputation as an increasing number of people from around the world discover us, usually through recommendations of friends or gourmet publications.

One of Canada's most important permanent collections is at the nearby McMichael Galleries. In a setting of 600 acres of parkland, it displays the world's largest collection of paintings by the Group of Seven.

The Doctor's House and Livery is easy to reach. It is a few miles north of Toronto via Highway 27, and only a few hundred feet off the highway, on the Nashville Road, in the village of Kleinburg. An alternate route is via Highway 400 to Major Mackenzie Drive, then west to Kleinburg.

The Doctor's House and Livery accepts these Credit Cards:

- AMERICAN EXPRESS   • CHARGEX / BANK AMERICARD
- DINERS CLUB   • MASTER CHARGE

Member:
- Canadian Restaurant Association
- Metropolitan Toronto Convention and Tourist Bureau

Closed Mondays

Telephone (416) 893-1615

The Doctor's house is one of the oldest residences in Kleinburg, dating back to 1867, Canada's Confederation year. It was built by John Dalziel on land described in the old deeds as "next to Mr. Donald's tavern," and willed on his death to his widow, Mary. Dr. James Stephenson, a bachelor doctor, lived there until 1877, when it was sold to another medical man, Dr. Thomas Harvey Robinson (1853-1929) who practised here for 52 years and who also served as health officer for the district.

Old Kleinburg residents still remember the doctor making his rounds faithfully on the coldest of winter nights. One of the two hitching posts used to tie up his buggy and horse — a grey named Dapple Dan — still stands at the gate. The Robinsons had four children, two of whom also became doctors. A daughter, Dr. Helen Robinson Beatty, lives in Toronto.

Old Canadian furnishings and medical memorabilia have been used throughout the house to evoke the past and remind us of the history of the village of Kleinburg when it was a stopping point for farmers bringing their produce to town. A tannery, harness-making shops, hotels and various other businesses lined the streets in those days while two mills, one on each branch of the Humber, ground up the grain. The village is near the portage route where the Indians and early explorers travelled from Lake Ontario to Lake Simcoe.

A plaque was erected at the Binder Twine Festival in 1968 at the restored cemetery just west of the Doctor's House, to commemorate Rev. and Mrs. E. A. Pearson, parents of Canada's former Prime Minister and Nobel Peace Prize winner, Lester B. Pearson. They lived down the street from Dr. Robinson from 1892-4, when Mr. Pearson preached in the Methodist Church on the hill.

The Livery was built in 1974 on the site of the original barn which was situated behind the Doctor's House. The Livery was designed after a typical stable of the 1800's. Its foot-square-beams are from British Columbia. Most of the pine furniture originated in the Kleinburg area and are all early Ontario antiques.

The Doctor's House & Livery

A historic site in Kleinburg, Ontario . . . now combining the quaintness of a country gift shop, The Doctor's House, with a spacious and handsome new restaurant, The Livery.

The Doctor's House actually was the home of two doctors successively during the late 1800's and the early 1900's, but, more recently, found fame in the area as an intimate, early-Ontario tea room.

The new Livery is built on the site of the long-gone barn which originally stood behind the Doctor's House and is designed after a stable of the period. It provides an authentic early-Ontario setting for relaxing, country-style dining, business lunches and special-occasion parties.

The authentically Canadian menu offers you a unique choice for luncheon or dinner. Among the specialties of the house are Ontario Pheasant, Saddle of Hare, Duckling and Veal. Many other Canadian and Continental specialties are included in the interesting menu, as well as a wide choice of steaks, roast beef and sea food in the traditional manner. A wide choice of imported and domestic wine is available at uncommonly reasonable prices.

For little people, and for those of modest appetite, special children's and "Grannies" portions are available, a unique feature of the Livery.

Many fine examples of antique pine cabinetry and pioneer farm tools are part of the early-Ontario theme of the Livery.

The Livery is a favourite for casual Après-ski dining.

The Livery is quiet, comfortable and relaxing. The construction and decor is of natural wood throughout, enhanced by pine cabinets and other antique reminders of country living.

The uncrowded Livery, with its muted, soft colours, subdued lighting and quiet elegance is popular with those who prefer

THE VALHALLA INN

This Scandinavian-styled Inn was the training ground for me in my early days, when I attended Ryerson and graduated in Hotel Resort and Restaurant Administration in 1965. Mr. Hans Bach, the general manager, hired me as a room service waiter, and later a waiter in the main dining room. The professional tuxedo-clad waiters were very smooth and well trained. I stood out like a sore thumb, but we all persevered. When Mr. and Mrs. Bach ate their meals in the dining room you could see my knees and serving tray shaking. One evening I dropped a tray full of main course dinners beside them. I wanted to crawl under the carpet, but both of them were very calm, cool and collected. They never did say anything, but I sure got hell from my maître d'. I guess that was all part of the training program. I worked as an intern, for nothing, for a month until I learned the night audit. Some mornings were a mess when I could not balance and people were checking in and out very early. I had the same night audit position in the Holiday Inn across the highway. Those National Cash Register machines were quite intimidating.

My favourite job was in breakfast room service on Saturday and Sunday mornings. I would start at about 6 AM and finish at about 11 AM. Within those two mornings, about ten hours in total, I would make about $75 to $100 in tips. I loved it because I treated it as a game. It was great to see how fast I was paid to leave those breakfasts and vanish. You see, a lot of romantic interludes took place on Friday and Saturday nights, which extended into next day morning breakfasts. The hotel had 160 guest rooms, which provided a lot of traffic and experiences! When you consider my first full time job paid me $110 weekly with $20 car allowance - that was a hell of a lot of money for my great experience.

Valhalla Inn Main Dining Room (ca. 1960s)

The Valhalla served great food and had an attractive Mermaid Lounge where you could see the hotel guests swimming. The lounge had windows through which people could view the antics and games people played. A lot of these people did not know they were on display and there were some embarrassing moments. This place served its purpose and is now a luxury condominium.

Bartender in Valhalla Inn's Mermaid Lounge

RISTORANTE PINOCCHIO

Pinocchio's was located at 4800 Dundas Street West at Islington in Etobicoke. The restaurant was opened in 1970 by Tony Giaquinto and Charly Sinagualia, and became a stalwart member of the community for forty three years. If you did not reserve your table you would be out of luck. There were not many first class Italian restaurants in Etobicoke in the 70s and 80s, but this was one of them. They served top quality milk fed veal and always had a great beef tenderloin on the menu. They served real scampis, not jumbo shrimps, and they made their own pasta. Unfortunately the restaurant closed in January of 2014 to make way for commercial development.

Caricature exterior sign at Ristorante Pinocchio

THE OLD MILL

The Old Mill at 21 Old Mill Road sits on the banks of the Humber River in what is known as the Kingsway area. It was an old, abandoned lumber mill that was revived by a developer named R. Home Smith, who wanted to build homes in the area. Building started in 1914. Old stone floors and hardwood were featured, however carpeting predominated in the newer additions. The Mill gave a hospitable air of a rural English inn, where excellent food was served by candlelight. Dancing was provided in the Victoria Ballroom to the Ellis McLintook Orchestra, who was one of the popular band leaders in the 50s, 60s and 70s. He played at most of the hotels in Toronto that offered dancing.

The Old Mill has changed hands over the years, but I remember it most when the Hodgsons owned it. This place was another great "necking" location in the West End near my house in the '50s and '60s. John Arena had a hand in management in the early 1970s, when the Mill had a capacity of roughly 600. The capacity was later expanded, with additions like a chapel added for weddings. The Hodgsons later sold it to the Kalmar family in 1991, who went on to develop the Constellation hotel complex. My family attended many pleasant functions at the Old Mill, and today it is a great Sunday and holiday brunch destination. It is also known as a jazz destination where many musicians performed.

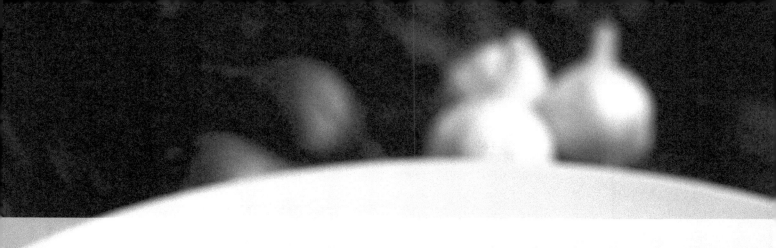

THE ITALIAN
CONNECTIONS

THE FLORENTINE COURT

The Florentine Court was located at 97 Church Street and is no longer in operation. When it was open, my old friend, Jimmy Lopresti, could be out front in the very relaxing and charming dining room or cooking in the kitchen at any time. Statues reminiscent of Florence, home of some of the world's greatest art treasures, were interspersed around tables set with red and blue tablecloths. The food was based on authentic central and northern Italian cuisine. One could choose from a seven course dinner or an a la carte menu. A good selection of veal, beef, chicken, and seafood was available. Jimmy served a very good striploin steak, which became a very popular item considering it was an Italian themed restaurant. The dessert speciality, called the Florentine Trifle, was served in a very large 400 oz. brandy snifter and was the most popular dessert in the house. It was made from two double layer commercial sponge cakes, 10 lbs of freshly-cleaned strawberries, 20 oz. of Marsala, 12 oz. of sweet sherry, 8 oz of brandy, 8 oz. of strega and 6 cups of fresh whipped cream, chilled—it was a fabulous treat. One of Jimmy's waiters named Charlie had a very humorous laugh that would echo throughout the dining room. As soon as that odd laugh was heard, everyone would start to laugh as well. It was infectious. It was also one of the highlights of the evening.

I was very fortunate in knowing Jimmy's family and got to know his brother Alfie, who had a restaurant in Hamilton. Alfie passed away far too early. He would invite me to come to Hamilton to have an early dinner with him and his family before they served dinner at the restaurant. That was very kind.

DOMENICS

Domenics was located at 173 Eglinton Avenue East and was another one of my favourites. I brought my wife there in the early 1980s for dinner on one of our first dates, and then to the Gardens for a hockey game. They served seven main veal entrees and a great selection of steaks. They were one of my biggest milk fed veal customers. Pork, lamb and chicken were also on the menu, as well as various seafood items. Domenics probably had the largest seafood platter for two in Toronto, besides La Castile in the West End. The restaurant had a Mediterranean atmosphere with stucco and many large plants. The lower level had a very relaxing ambiance, where a grand piano provided entertainment and played requests. The owner died in the early '90s and the restaurant was never the same; it closed shortly thereafter.

OLD ANGELO'S

Old Angelo's was the oldest Italian restaurant in Toronto. The restaurant was called Angelo's and started in 1922, as stated on their match book. It was renamed Old Angelo's in 1938, located at 45 Elm Street. I met the chef, Raeffele Crosato, a tall, very personable and handsome man, in 1969.

His pasta dishes ranged from spaghetti, gnocchi, tagliatelli, rigatoni, cannelloni, lasagne and ravioli selections. There were eight beef steak items, five veal items, three chicken items and six fish items to satisfy their patrons' tastes. The old world ambiance was provided by wrought iron and velvet dividers. The restaurant was dedicated to the culinary excellence that was established the day it was opened. The restaurant was sold to Domenic and Connie Ciccocioppo in 1983. It was renamed Oro. They were previously the owners of Bumpkin's.

Old Angelo's Dining Room (ca. 1960s)

Old Angelo's exterior (ca. late 1970s)

NOODLES

Noodles opened in 1972 at 60 Bloor Street West. The entrance was actually a few steps north of Bloor Street on Bay Street, which was a little confusing. It was opened by executive chef Herbert Sonzogni and inspired by George Minden, the owner of the Windsor Arms Hotel. Herbert had a profound understanding of northern Italian cooking from his formative years in Italy. Northern Italian cooking features delicate cream based sauces instead of the tomato based sauces used in the south. The restaurant was very modern in appearance and displayed chrome, glass and leather with a large pasta kettle in the middle of the open kitchen. All food, including bread, was made in-house. A great performance was put into preparing and serving each meal. The place offered ample meat choices: beef, lamb, veal, osso bucco, chicken, fish and seafood. Amazing pastries, desserts and even deep fried ice cream were offered. In 1985 Noodles was sold to Dante Rota, another executive chef of the Windsor Arms Hotel, his wife, Rina, and his son, Carlo (now an accomplished actor), who helped Dante immensely. Sadly, Noodles closed in 1990.

TASTEFUL FISH AND SEAFOOD DESTINATIONS

THE MERMAID SEAFOOD HOUSE

This restaurant was advertised as an exclusive seafood house, meaning that it did not serve any meat products. It was located at 724 Bay Street, near Gerrard, and was opened in 1965 as a small, 36 seat restaurant, but grew threefold after achieving popularity. The Mermaid was then divided into three separately themed dining rooms and had a distinct Scandinavian flavour. This very busy place had to be one of the best in Toronto, and reservations were a must. The Mermaid offered over forty varieties of seafood. Hors' D'Oeuvres offered smoked salmon, shrimp, steamed mussels or clams, 5 different oyster selections, and escargots. Soups offered were fish chowder, oyster stew, lobster bisque, clam chowder, and conch.

Delectable shellfish entrees ranged from seven delicious lobster choices, three Alaska king crab options, langostinos, four shrimp selections, scallops, and Danish scampis. You could choose the Mermaid Platter, which contained steamed lobster, king and Alaska crab legs, Danish scallops, lobster tails, langostinos, mussels and clams. Fish choices offered were halibut, salmon, Florida snapper, eel, Dover sole, arctic char, cod, flounder, Georgian Bay white fish, Dover plaice and rainbow trout. Frog's legs were also available. Specialties of the house were curried eel and Danish style cabillard, which was poached cod. A great finishing touch to any of these wonderful dishes would be a Danish Akvavit or two.

THE FISHERMAN'S WHARF—PIER 1

The Fisherman's Wharf, located on Adelaide Street between University and York, was a noted seafood restaurant. If you think the Mermaid's menu, with forty items, had a lot to offer, Pier 1 had sixty items, including a large selection of lobster, and covered over twelve pages. The decor here was like dining on a luxury ocean liner, and service was on two levels and open in the center. A massive sparkling chandelier hung in that open space for all to admire. The waiters were dressed as ship's officers. All that was missing was the ocean and a slight lilt to the building. They served a filet mignon for non-fish lovers, thank you kindly. They catered to the after dinner and after theatre crowd, and provided dancing as well as a limited menu.

DISTINCTIVE
HOTELS

THE KING EDWARD HOTEL

The King Edward Hotel opened in 1903 at 37 King Street East at Victoria. Six stories were built in 1901 and two more were added in 1902. The Oak Room was obviously designed to meet the needs of business travellers. Frescoes of hunting scenes and oak panelling gave the room the aura of a private club. The Pickwick Tavern was a gentlemen's bar with an old English ambiance, and, in my opinion, made the finest steak and kidney pie anywhere in the world. I loved going there. The Times Square Room was another

popular stop. The hotel was designed to be the center of entertainment for the city's upper middle class and social elite. The hotel's design was modeled after the Waldorf Astoria and the Plaza in New York.

Before 1900, Toronto society rarely dined out in the evening or entertained away from home. Private clubs provided for members, but not for the members' wives. The "Palm Room" was where tea and light refreshments were served. The second floor accommodated banquet rooms of the finest houses in Toronto. The "Victorian Room" was the hotel's jewel and was described as "elegant enough in style to serve as the boudoir of a pompadour were its dimensions not so vast." Additions and redecorating were made in

1917. During the 1920's several hotels were built in Toronto, but only the Royal York (1929) presented any serious challenge in appearance and competition. In 1979 new owners, working with the Trust House Forte hotel group from England, managed the King Edward and completely restored the hotel. The hotel was almost demolished at this time. The 470 rooms were converted to 322 larger rooms and 30 large suites. The Oak Room was demolished and many changes were made. At this time I met Dante Rota, who decided shortly thereafter that he wasn't the man for this place and moved on. John Higgins, a very likeable and superb executive chef, was a mainstay at the hotel for years. Today the hotel still symbolizes the lifestyle and standards of a period that has all but disappeared.

THE PRINCE GEORGE HOTEL

The Prince George Hotel at King and York was another one of those hotels that contributed to the early landscape of downtown Toronto. The Embers Steak House featured charcoal broiled steaks and prime ribs of roast beef, as well as the house specialty of baked Canadian fresh lobster. The Pyramid Room provided nightly entertainment in a richly Egyptian flavoured room. It is unfortunate that hotels like the Prince George closed to make way for the modern redevelopment of the downtown core. Modern hotels replaced these old structures, but the charm and dignity were never replaced.

THE LORD SIMCOE

The Lord Simcoe Hotel was one of the "original six," located downtown at 150 King Street West at University Avenue, and had 725 guest rooms. Single rooms sold for $12.50 per night in the '60s. The most important feature I remember about the hotel is that it contained the Lord Simcoe Art Gallery and introduced me to Wolfgang Schilbach's artwork. The Flaming Grill was an open grill concept that had an atmosphere of contemporary sophistication. A popular feature was dancing on Friday and Saturday evenings. The Captain's Table was a popular grill room, where roast beef and seafood were served in the atmosphere of an 18th century ship. The Beau Nash Room was a smartly decorated cocktail lounge that was closed on Saturdays and Sundays. The Sentry Box was a unique bar that had waiters dressed in colourful military costumes. Again, although the hotel provided Toronto with many stories and was an integral part of Toronto's hotel history, the Lord Simcoe closed in 1962. I'm just very sorry that I did not buy a few more paintings at the Lord Simcoe Art Gallery.

THE ROYAL YORK

The Royal York Hotel was a gem in the Canadian Pacific Hotel chain, and the largest hotel in the British Commonwealth. The Canadian Pacific hotels, such as the Royal York, Château Frontenac in Quebec City, Château Champlain in Montreal, the Empress in Vancouver, Banff Springs and the Château Lake Louise in the Alberta Rockies were all part of the CP conglomerate before they were broken up. The Royal York was opened in 1929. One of the hotel's clients in 1932 was Winston Churchill. In the late 1950s a 17 storey east wing was added to provide more than a thousand guestrooms. The hotel had everything: a roof top garden, a small hospital, a library and a concert hall. It was also very opulent, with beautiful hand-painted ceilings, crystal chandeliers and magnificent wall hangings.

The Royal York's connection to Union Station turned it into a daily breakfast destination. With the addition of the GO Train system, Union Station was huge and many executives coming to work daily, and other travellers, would eat breakfast across the street at the hotel. At least 500 people a day would do breakfast—not including meetings and conventions. When I originally started in the meat business with Swift and Company, the hotel would go through 200 boxes (or a ton of bacon) weekly. It was also the first hotel to organically grow their herbs, fruits and vegetables.

The Imperial Room, located inside the hotel, was not only a high end dinner and supper dining room, but also served breakfast and lunch. Dancing was offered seven days a week with supper in The Venetian Room; the Princess Lounge and the Arcadia Coffee Shop were other eating outlets in the hotel. Wealthy families in Toronto would consider the Royal York their second home. Marcel Didier was the executive chef at the time I came into the picture, and Danny Samyn was the Director of Purchasing. I got to know Louis Jannetta later on in the 1980s, and attended his fabulous retirement party in the Imperial Room at the Royal York Hotel. What a turnout!

John Cordeau was a very gifted and remarkable chef who made many positive changes at the Royal York. Another good friend, Ed Pietras, worked as an elevator operator back when elevators were not as easy to operate as they are now. This was a part time job because he was still going to school. He was the guy in the white starched shirt uniform. Did he ever have stories to tell about the night time shenanigans that went on during those years!

In 1962, the Black Night Room, a formal night club dining room with a medieval ambiance, opened and became very popular. It attracted professional athletes, foreign dignitaries and international actors, and featured performances from numerous entertainers. For over four decades, starting in the '40s, all the National Hockey League teams stayed at the Royal York. In 1965, the Imperial Room was redesigned and expanded to accommodate more people. In the years that followed, much reconstruction modernized the "Grand Dame." As mentioned in another chapter, the Benihana Steak House was a significant customer of mine. They bought only the highest quality of US choice beef and asked for US prime when it was available. They were a franchise separate entity in the Royal York complex, but in the early '90s they were taken over by the hotel.

My mother, Mary, worked there as a pantry girl in the late 1930s and early '40s. The hotel was used as a location for the movie The Killing Fields in 1984, although the majority of the film was shot in Thailand. The Cinderella Man (2005) and Mr. Magorium's Wonder Emporium (2007), along with several other movies, have also been filmed there.

THE WESTBURY HOTEL

The Westbury Hotel was a six hundred room twin tower, centrally located in downtown Toronto, a slap shot away from Maple Leaf Gardens and not too far from Eaton's department store (now known as the Eaton Centre). It was owned by the US Knott Hotel Group. The hotel had a history of exceptional people in the kitchen, starting with George Gourbault, Tony Roldan, Joe Vonlanthan, Fred Reindl, Herbert Sonzogni, Horst Fabian, Gunther Guglemier and Gerry Nadon. Mr. Gourbault moved on to the Inn on the Park. Tony Roldan moved on to the Harbour Castle. Joe Vonlanthan became the executive chef at the Constellation Hotel. Fred Reindl became chef at the Hyatt Regency. Herbert Sonzogni took over at the Windsor Arms. Horst Fabian also went to the Inn on the Park. Gunther Guglemier stayed the longest and I'm happy to say I got to know him the most of all. Gerry Nadon moved on to become a partner at Oliffe's Butcher Shop, which to this day caters to Rosedale's finest. Sam and Ben Gundy now own and manage Oliffe's.

The Westbury Dining Room became one of the top five restaurants in the city in the late '50s and '60s and gained five stars. No ingredients were spared to attain a first class dining room. This was truly a fabulous world class destination. All sorts of flambées, game birds, you name it; the Westbury served it and that made their reputation. Fresh meats and fish were the order of the day. No frozen products were used. Fresh calves' liver was a specialty. "Scampis in Love" originated at the Westbury. Again, the Westbury would only use top quality US choice and US prime aged beef. The Normandy Room (lively and honky tonk fun) and the Polo Lounge, served drinks, but were closed on Sundays to conform to liquor laws of the province. The Sky Lounge, on the 17th floor, offered a great view and a great drink. Would you believe that the rate of a single room started at $18.50 per night in the '70s?

THE PARK PLAZA

The Park Plaza was indeed one of the original high end "six" in Toronto in the '40s, '50s and early '60s. The original six were; Walker House, Lord Simcoe, Westbury, Park Plaza, the King Edward and the Royal York. It was located at the corner of Avenue Road and Bloor Street at 4 Avenue Road. The Park Plaza had two main dining rooms and three cocktail lounges. The dining facilities were the Roof Dining Room on the 18th floor, and the Prince Arthur Dining Room on the lobby level. Both of these dining venues served afternoon tea daily from 3 to 5 pm. The "SRO Bar" featured a sophisticated lunch time treat of hot roast beef sandwiches on Italian bread with spicy baked beans served by gorgeous waitresses dressed in 'hot pants.' Cocktails were served in the Plaza Room, the Roof Lounge and the Prince Arthur Lounge. Peter Appleyard entertained in most of the lounges in the hotel. Seven other banquet rooms were available for special parties. The popular "Murray's" operated the coffee shop on the street level.

The hotel served only the finest US choice and US prime beef. The chef was Fred Stahaly, and the General Manager was an American, Ed Shaughnessy, who was a guest lecturer at Ryerson in the hospitality faculty. I would see him three or four times during the year. I caught up with Mr. Stahaly at Winston's later on. My best memories of the Park Plaza were the ones of going to enjoy Peter Appleyard and his music on the roof and having a few drinks. I met up with him many years later and got him to play at my sixtieth birthday party. Joining him were John Sherwood (piano), Neil Swainson (bass) and Reg Schwager (guitar). Swainson and Schwager also played with the great George Shearing. What a blast!

Years past until I met Joan Monfaredi, a chef and fine lady at Telfers. She had come into Toronto from the West and was looking for work. She was overqualified to work at Telfers and wound up at the Park Plaza, which had become the Park Hyatt. Another one of my regrets was not getting to know her better, but she did find another supplier who served her well over the years. You can't win them all!

THE CHELSEA INN

The original structure where the Chelsea Inn, at 33 Gerrard Street, was started as an apartment building by a German developer who ran out of money. The building could not be finished and a company called Markborough Developments, who were developing the College Park complex, bought the site for almost nothing. Markborough owned the Chelsea Inn until it was sold to a group called Great Eagle Holdings. Delta Hotels never owned the complex, but managed it for some time. The hotel opened in October of 1975, with 250 rooms to begin with; far too small. By 1977 the hotel had converted to 975 hotel rooms from the apartment complex they had started with. By 1990 the hotel had grown to 1600 guest rooms and suites on 27 floors under the Great Eagle Hotels Canada Ltd. The hotel's infrastructure always suffered because of limited service space in relation to the size of the structure. The hotel had three restaurants. The Spotted Cow had 90 seats and was a cafeteria style self-serve facility; the Kitchen Garden was adequate; and Whittles was a feature dining room. The Kitchen Garden was later incorporated into Whittles. The hotel was described as intimate and cozy, like an English country inn in the heart of Toronto.

I started dealings with the Chelsea Inn in 1979 when Domenic Zoffranieri was there as sous chef; he became the executive chef from 1979 to 1992. He was 26 years old—pretty young to be in such a responsible position. He apprenticed at the Hyatt, so he had some good training. Domenic started something pretty unique at the Chelsea. He had us bring in grade A4 Canadian carcasses of beef. That grade A4 was comparable to the present day Canadian prime. We would stamp the carcasses at the slaughter house and then deliver the long loins and the short loins to the hotel. The hotel would butcher that product into the cuts they would use. Some dry-ageing also went into the process at the hotel. That way they could control the quality they wanted. I would say that the Chelsea was the first hotel to have that kind of butcher facility in Toronto. All other hotels bought what we called boxed beef, in that they purchased striploins, tenderloins, top butts and 7-bone ribs all ready to be used. There was not a lot of Canadian A4 grade beef available, so we had to select carefully. Joe Dermastja was a master at that, and did a superb job of selection. He did the same for the milk fed veal and specialty meats. The veal livers would be selected in the morning, and, when they were delivered in the early afternoon, they would still be warm—that was fresh! That does not happen now!

Raymond Zyvatkauskas took over as executive chef from Dominic in 1992, and stayed until 1998. Bruce Kowalchuk, a very close friend and executive chef of the Harbour Sixty Steakhouse, apprenticed at the Chelsea Inn starting in 1986. Bruce was the executive chef that Harbour Sixty Steakhouse had up until his death in November, 2013. I also spent some productive years dealing with Ann Lytle, the Chelsea's purchasing agent.

HYATT REGENCY

The Hyatt led the explosion of Toronto hotel development in 1972. It was downtown, at 21 Avenue Road and Yorkville Avenue. The hippie coffee houses and beatnik hangouts were giving way to high end eateries and expensive boutiques, so this was a great location. The hotel was designed in the unique Hyatt fashion, featuring luxurious decor, huge atrium lobbies, convention amenities and a high end dining room called "Truffles." Most dishes were garnished with truffles in that room. "Truffles" are grown in the Perigord region of France underground in the roots of oak trees. This mushroom-like vegetable is scarce and very expensive. Fred Reindl from the Walker House was the executive chef, joined by Hans Kocaurek, food and beverage director, also from the Walker House. Franco Prevedello was the banquet manager. "Truffles" raised the bar to new heights in fine dining in Toronto. The service was second to none, and the wine cellar was excellent the wine selection was excellent.

The dining room was something out of a classic movie, with its original gaslights, stylish and lovely Italian fabrics, Royal Doulton china and accessories. There was a magnificent tapestry from France that dated back to the 16th century. The hotel was immaculate and fashionably furnished and was certainly world class.

One morning as I was coming in through the back entrance to see the chef, I caught young Elton John with a Los Angeles Dodgers jacket on, running out to avoid fans. He could really move! Mind you, he was forty years younger than he is today. The Hyatt Regency certainly would attract celebrities, entertainers and dignitaries. The Hyatt would become the Four Seasons Yorkville in 1977 and continue on as one of the supreme hotels in Toronto.

THE INN ON THE PARK

The Café De L'Auberge was the elegant centerpiece at the Inn on the Park. Georges Chaignet was the executive chef and Ian Munro was the general manager. Built in 1963, this hotel was not located in the downtown Toronto area where most explosive growth took place. The Inn was located at 1100 Eglinton Avenue East at Leslie Street. Again, this hotel was very classy and was expensive to visit. Each dish on the beautiful menu was described in detail and was a gastronomique experience. Georges Chaignet earned the distinguished silver medal of the Chaîne des Rôtisseurs, awarded for the highest culinary achievement in the world. At one time, he was the only North American chef to be so honoured. On his eighteen page menu, appetizers included mussels, shrimp, escargot, oysters, crab legs, a selection of pâté, smoked fish, lobster and quail eggs. Specialties of the house were veal kidney, calf's sweet breads, veal medallions, saddle of rabbit and lamb, hare, sirloin steak and beef tenderloin. The Inn on the Park always used the finest of US choice and US prime beef and lamb. Fish and seafood included lobster. Game birds were the real specialty of the house, with entrees that included pheasant, duck, quail and Guinea fowl. Desserts were spectacular and were served from a trolley. Dancing followed for a memorable evening. The wine cellar was extensive and first class. Dinner for two with a good wine would cost $60 to $75, and was well worth the cost. The Buttery, another dining area in the hotel, served a very classy lunch time menu, but was expensive. Of course, as time passed into the '80s and '90s and later, many changes occurred in the hotel industry and this hotel lost popularity. It was eventually demolished in 2006.

L'HOTEL

Many people did not realize that L'Hotel was a CN hotel before the CN hotels were taken over by CP Hotels. This hotel was built on land owned by the crown corporation, Canadian National, on Front Street West adjacent to the CN Tower property. It was built in the early 1980s and did not have a long life as L'Hotel. The CN hotel chain had their head office in Montreal, Quebec. The president of the CN Hotel organization wanted a French flavour to the name of their new hotel and called it L'Hotel. Being located in an Anglophone city, this did pose somewhat of a problem. Anglophones, American and international travelers had a problem pronouncing the name. They called it "L. Hotel" and not "L'Hotel." Be that as it may, the hotel got stuck with that moniker. It was interconnected to the Metropolitan Convention Centre and was quite convenient to people attending trade shows or conventions.

John Makela (plant manager) and Ron Chapchuk at J.J. Derma Meats Christmas Party at L'Hotel

J.J. Derma Meats had their first Christmas party at L'Hotel before the hotel actually opened. Because we were to be major suppliers to the hotel when they opened, the chef at that time, Claude Gambin, allowed us to soft-open the hotel before Christmas. What a fabulous affair! Really, no expense was spared and the employees had a very remarkable experience. My family, including my mother and father, my wife and two children, saw dad dressed up as Santa Claus who gave Christmas presents to very happy employees. After a short time the hotel became the Crowne Plaza.

THE SKYLINE HOTEL

The Skyline Hotel opened its doors in October 1954, five days before Hurricane Hazel (not the mayor!) hit Toronto with a fury. The property was the very first hotel on the airport strip, opening with twenty three guest rooms and a men's beverage room. This hotel was opened by Bill and Ted Hodgson, who were the owners of the Toronto Argonaut football team. Bill Hodgson went on to own the Constellation Hotel, the Old Mill and the Doctor's House after John MacEachern's tenure. This hotel has grown 25 fold to the 450 room full service hotel that it is today, at the crossroads of highways 427 and Dixon Road. To think that this hotel was built in the middle of nowhere in a field on Dixon Road, and to see where it is today, in the middle of the city proper, is unimaginable. The airport was nowhere near the complex it is today, so the Skyline's facilities were very convenient. It was also the first hotel to secure a liquor license in Etobicoke.

The hotel has catered to many famous celebrities and dignitaries, such as Prime Minister Pierre Trudeau, Elton John and Tom Jones. The Henry VIII room was an excellent dining room that served continental cuisine. The Cloud Room offered dancing and entertainment. During the '60s and '70s, "Diamond Lil's," a saloon located in the hotel, was one of the most popular beer drinking spots in Toronto, featuring regular performances by Vanda King and Kitty Meredith. The pub and the Rendevous Lounger were the other two outlets. One of my favourite singers, Vic Franklin, was also featured at the Skyline, but what with Frank Sinatra, Paul Anka, and Tony Bennett being so popular, the chances of him succeeding as a singer were very slim, although he was a Toronto favourite. A very good friend of mine, Ted Herriott, who was an accomplished drummer, played there frequently with Jimmy Namaro and the Greg and Gino Antonacci band. Phil McKellar, a local jazz disc jockey, known as that "feller McKellar," was very popular and hosted many shows out of the Skyline.

Runway 23, a bar that sat atop the Skyline, was a stopover for many travellers in and out of the airport. The Skyline also housed a health club, which stood separately from the hotel and was operated by Ralph Gardiner. It was home to many of my friends who would frequent the facilities before and after work. Unfortunately I never joined because I was far too healthy and fit at that time.

Henry VIII Dining room

THE SHERATON HOTEL

The Sheraton opened in 1972 and was owned by a very large American multinational combine called I.T.T. The hotel was a massive building taking up four acres of land in the middle of downtown Toronto, interconnected to the Toronto City Hall. This huge structure, the second largest hotel in Toronto after the Royal York, was designed for mammoth conventions of up to 10,000 people. The banquet kitchen could serve twenty different function rooms. The 20,000 square foot ballroom could seat 2,000 people. The Sheraton had eleven bars and restaurants and also a rooftop lounge. My friend Hans Stuerzen Becher served as executive banquet chef for a time. The men's health club, located in the hotel and called the Cambridge Club, was a good customer of ours. The dining room was the perfect place to hold my 60th birthday brunch. The barber shop at the Sheraton Centre served me well for 30 years. The hotel was home to many labour and industry meetings because of the parking, shopping and accommodations offered there. It was truly a city within a city, and it is still a very busy place.

Peter Appleyard performing at Sheraton's Cambridge Club (2001)

Walker House Hotel, exterior (1970)

THE WALKER HOUSE HOTEL

The Walker House opened in the late 1800s at 121 Front Street, west of York Street. It was a very simple railway hotel, owned by the Wright family. It was located across the street from Toronto's Union Station and was the oldest hotel in Canada. Years later, in the late 1950s, this hotel was completely renovated into a Swiss, Austrian and German-themed dining establishment: The Franz Josef Supper Club, the Rathskeller, and the Swiss Bear Lounge. These restaurants became instant successes because they each appealed to a different dining experience. Dining here was truly a new adventure in an old world atmosphere. The Living Room (a lounge) and Granny's (a disco) were added later.

The Franz Josef presented famous Austrian cuisine, with dinner, dancing and entertainment nightly in an authentic Viennese atmosphere. The Swarovski chandeliers, silk wallpaper, French service and flambé cuisine also presented a French overtone. The international gourmet menu changed every two to three months, and a chanteuse entertained twice nightly. The room had the best selection of Rhine, Moselle, Burgundy and Château wines in the city. They were the first restaurant to serve wild hare and wild boar on the menu, and had the best vichyssoise in town. The Rathskeller presented superb German food and beverages in a friendly, old world environment and music was played nightly on a zither by Robert Bushman. The restaurant, with its check board red tablecloths and stained glass, had a very Bavarian decor. They served Schnitzel, Sauerbraten, Rolladen, Kessler, red cabbage and specialty called "Feisbein," which were pork hocks (German soul food). The Swiss Bear presented a congenial Swiss alpine hideaway, with furnishings imported from Switzerland. You could go there before and after dinner hours. Beer was served in steins in both the Rathskeller and the Swiss Bear. The Walker House chefs made a dessert soufflé called "Sulzberger Hockle," which

Rathskeller

THE WALKER HOUSE HOTEL, TORONTO

Ontario

Canada's First Wine Auction

ONE OF THE FINEST
GERMAN WINE CELLARS IN NORTH AMERICA

will be sold at auction by the

LIQUOR CONTROL BOARD OF ONTARIO

and through its agent

WARD-PRICE LIMITED, AUCTIONEERS

This cellar, formerly the property of

TORONTO'S WALKER HOUSE HOTEL

is renowned for its German wines but also features

A FINE SELECTION OF FRENCH PRODUCTS

ALL BIDDERS

must be registered and of the age of majority in order to obtain a purchasing number
and must provide suitable credentials if they wish to pay for purchases by cheque.
Sales to the public are subject to a 10 per cent Ontario Retail Sales Tax.

ALL SALES ARE FINAL

Licensees are welcome to bid but will be subject to a 12 per cent gallonage fee.
No credit cards will be accepted.

Catalogues are priced at $5.00 each and admit two persons to the auction.
They are available at the Liquor Control Board of Ontario, 55 Lakeshore Blvd. East
and at Ward-Price Limited, Auctioneers, 112 St. Clair Ave. West.
The auction, involving more than

10,000 BOTTLES OF WINE

will be held in

THE LIBRARY, CASA LOMA

at

7 P.M., WEDNESDAY, OCTOBER 6, 1976

Further information on the auction and purchase of catalogues is available at

(416) 868-0973

Richard Burton and Elizabeth Taylor at the Rathskeller in the Walker House Hotel (ca. 1960s)

was baked and dressed with a vanilla sauce. In its prime the Rathskeller and the Franz Joseph would serve over one thousand patrons on a Saturday night. When Ed Mirvish held his opening night celebration for the Royal Alex, it was at the Franz Josef.

There were three chefs responsible for the success of the Walker House. The first was Ted Linden, who opened the Walker House; Fred Reindl who succeeded Mr. Linden; and Gunther Guglmier. I regret that I never had the pleasure of meeting Ted Linden, but I did meet Fred Reindl, who became the Executive Chef of the Hyatt Regency, and Gunther, whom I became friends with at the Westbury Hotel. I became a faithful supplier to the Westbury and I cherish those years.

Mr. George Schwab was the first General Manager of the Walker House, and my good friend Peter Hackenberger later succeeded him. I met Peter in the late 1960s. Peter, up until my retirement in June of 2013, still purchased his beef tenderloins and roast beef from me. Peter went on from the Walker House to the Royal Bank organization and managed their dining rooms. He then went on to become the General Manager of the private National Club on Bay Street. He has been very helpful in the writing of this story, and every time we meet there are stories galore that we share and enjoy.

(Left to right) George Schwab, Marlene Dietrich, and Peter Hackenberger at the Walker House Hotel (ca. 1960s)

THE CONSTELLATION HOTEL

The Constellation Hotel was built in 1962 on Dixon Road next to the airport. It was previously built to accommodate conferences, small conventions and tradeshows. The hotel grew from 120 rooms to 900, and many claimed it was too large. Single room rates started at $17 per night. The original partners who built the Constellation were Ben Dunkelman and Alex Hacker. I got to know Mr. and Mrs. Dunkelman and their family through the restaurant they owned called "Dunkelman's," and I spoke with them quite frequently. Mr. Dunkelman was a distinguished war hero, who was quite approachable and very cordial.

Joe Vonlanthen was the executive chef who taught many apprentices who went on to great careers. Over his thirty years, three hundred apprentices served under him. He attended Escoffier meetings faithfully and was quite a personable fellow. The Burgundy Room was the main dining room and, at one time, was advertised as the only top rated dining room in the airport area. Joe cooked for numerous celebrities over the years, including Muhammad Ali and former Prime Minister Trudeau. Joe passed away in 2013 at the end of a masterful career. I understand that the SARS epidemic in Toronto led to the closure of the Constellation. The hotel was never the same. It was abandoned and finally demolished in 2011.

THE SUTTON PLACE & BISTRO 990

The Sutton Place was opened in 1967 and was originally a resident-friendly rental building that was renovated to accommodate the growing entertainment business in Toronto, which accounted for 35% of the Sutton Place room rentals. Its original claim to fame came from a shocking bombing that occurred three months after it opened. On November 10th, a bomb was placed under the mattress in a room occupied by stock promoter Myer-Rush. He had stolen $30-million from underworld figures and they employed a prostitute to plant the bomb and extract their revenge on Rush. The bomb exploded, but did not kill Rush, as he eventually recovered from his injuries.

The Sutton Place eventually became part of the Kempinski chain of hotels that was not a very successful venture. The hotel became the home away from home for many popular movie stars and world class political figures. Celebrities such as Sophia Loren, Peter Ustinov, Lorne Green, Tony Curtis, Gregory Peck, George Burns, Marlon Brando, Trevor Howard and Michael Jackson all stayed there. In terms of major public figures, Pierre Trudeau, King Hussein of Jordan, Helmut Kohl, Ahmad Shah of Pahang and Sir Edmund Hillary all stayed at the Sutton. Neils Kjeldsen served as executive chef for a period, and a very young Mark McEwen passed through as executive chef for a short time. The main dining room, the Sansouci, and the chic Alexandra Bar served the guests well. In earlier times the Royal Hunt Room served a magnificent brunch buffet for $3.50 per person on Sundays. Stop 33, the famed rooftop lounge, was one of Toronto's most popular.

Having a conference center, the hotel attracted the Toronto International Film Festival and became the place to stay. When Three Men and a Baby was filmed in Toronto in 1987, actor Ted Danson took up residence at the Sutton for several months and routinely hosted large dinner parties while residing there. The Sutton Place became the Festival's official headquarters. Hans Gerhardt, who had been at the Walker House, Hyatt Regency and the Sheraton finally arrived as the manager of the Sutton Place in 1986. He had probably met more celebrities from all walks of life than any other hotel manager in history.

Across the street, the Bistro 990 also became an important restaurant in the early '90s due to the increasing importance and popularity of TIFF. Bistro 990 was opened in 1988, and took its name from its address on Bay Street. Tom Kristenbrun (amongst other things a one-time Argonaut, chartered accountant and El Mocambo proprietor) was the owner of Bistro 990 and I was fortunate to cultivate a relationship with him and Ricardo Roque, an extremely talented chef at the bistro. With the addition of Alfred Caron as the General Manager, who came over from the CN Tower, the Bistro became the most popular restaurant amongst celebrities and movie stars during the period of the film festival. The 'Meg Ryan roast chicken' was the signature dish, a name developed after the actress allegedly requested it be delivered daily to a nearby film set. However, steak and other beef options were always in demand. With the relocation of the film festival headquarters in 2010, Bistro 990's business suffered tremendously and it closed in 2012. Ricardo Roque and Ricardo Sousa, a waiter at Bistro 990, are now partners in a wonderful restaurant in the Yorkville area called Crème Brasserie.

As for the nearby Sutton Place, it too suffered similar turmoil as its neighbour. After changing ownership in 1993, it was closed in 2012. The Lanterra Development acquired the property and it is being turned into a condo development called the Britt.

GEMS

THE ORIGINAL MÖVENPICK

The original Mövenpick opened in the early 1980s at 165 York Street under the direction of Chef Joe Bruger. Joe came from the Mövenpick organization in Switzerland, and was very receptive to my recommendations and general advice. Mövenpick boasted one of the largest and best buffets at that time, and could not handle the volume of patrons on Sundays. The restaurant was laid out in a multi-level seating arrangement, which provided a very comfortable atmosphere and lots of privacy.

The Mövenpick had proposed to purchase 1000 beef tenderloins at a certain price over a certain period of time. When all the replies came back, Canada Packers came in about three dollars per pound cheaper than us. I told Joe it was a very good deal and that it was impossible for me to make any money at all, and for him to take this contract immediately. Joe followed instructions on their tenderloins, but gave me most of his other meat orders. In a short period the tenderloin contract could not be fulfilled, and I was given it at a higher price. Mövenpick was a huge user of various meat products and proved to be a very important customer of mine. They used so much meat that they employed their own butcher and had their own butcher facility. They also had their own bakery and produced fabulous desserts.

I got married there to my wife, Florence, on May 17th, 1985. Chef Gunther Lorsheidt presided. Mr. and Mrs. Jorge Reichert succeeded to the throne and grew the company through tough times. I was very happy to have been part of those earlier and formative years.

THE MARS

The Mars open style kitchen at 432 College Street, just east of Bathurst Street, billed itself as serving "food out of this world." It was definitely home comfort food served at its best. They had cabbie and police personnel as their main customers, but generally appealed to a wide cross section of people. They were one of the first all-day-breakfast restaurants. They made a famous corned beef hash and served some of the best chopped liver, even better than the Jewish delis. They were known for their fabulous rice pudding and their very popular bran muffins, which they baked all day and sold for 10 cents. There was no excuse for not being "regular" if you lived in the neighbourhood. I took my family there quite frequently in the '60s. The place hardly ever closed and seemed always packed because of the limited space. It could not have been more than 30 feet at its widest.

GEORGE'S SPAGHETTI HOUSE

With the pizza craze starting in the '50s, Georges and Vesuvios on Dundas Street West in the Junction had the best pizza bar. George's was at Sherbourne and Dundas Street East. For a young teenager who lived in Etobicoke like me, it was a long way to come for a pizza, but it was cheap, and there was no traffic gridlock like there is now. It was a joy to come downtown to enjoy the fabulous pizza. My favourite was a #17 large with mushrooms and pepperoni. The pizza even tasted great cold the next day, so I would always order one to go. The cheese they used was rich and very flavourful. I have not tasted a cheese like that since then. The pepperoni was the IL Primo quality, not that cheap filler stuff. The mushrooms they used were small and button sized. After she had a #17 pizza, my mother used that kind of mushroom for her gravies and other uses for years. During the '50s and early '60s I attended Royal York Collegiate and, I swear, I must have introduced 20 percent of the student body to George's. The restaurant had great ambiance, with red table cloths and candles stuck into Chianti wine bottles. Stan was my favourite waiter. Doug Cole was the gracious host and owner.

Upstairs was Castle George, which had a more elaborate menu and hosted numerous jazz shows. George's was one of Toronto's early jazz centers and was a favourite place for local jazz musicians, like Moe Koffman, Archie Alleyne (one of the owners of the Underground Railroad.) and also many US performers. The Toronto Maple Leaf hockey team ate their pre-game daily pasta lunches there when they were in town in the '60s, as well as when they last won the Stanley Cup. There must have been something special in the pasta!

UNITED BAKERS

United Bakers originally opened in 1912 and has been family owned ever since. It was founded by Aaron and Sarah Ladovsky, and is now run by their grandchildren, Phil and Ruth. It started at 338 Spadina Avenue, north of Dundas. Years later it moved up to 506 Lawrence Avenue West, near Bathurst Street. You can order virtually anything except for meat. It is a dairy restaurant and a great meeting place for families. On Saturday and Sunday mornings you can see anywhere from six to twenty people gathering together for a meal. On the menu are wonderfully filling soups, such as borscht, chicken, pea, barley and matzah-ball. Gefilte fish is a given. In this very health conscious world their fresh salads have become very popular, but so have the blintzes and French toast. They have a large take-out selection of various foods, and their menu is very extensive.

Rose Lieberman, Rose [Hanford?] Green and Aaron and Sarah Ladovsky in front of United Bakers Restaurant (1920).

United Bakers Dairy Restaurant, exterior Lawrence Avenue location (1986)

THE ORIGINAL

UNITED BAKERS
DAIRY RESTAURANT
Downtown

MENU
Delightfully Delicious
Dairy Dishes

Downtown	**Uptown**
338 Spadina Ave.	506 Lawrence Ave. West
Toronto	*in the Lawrence Plaza*
593-0697	789-0519

A La Carte

PRICES DO NOT INCLUDE ONTARIO PROVINCIAL SALES TAX
CASHIER WILL ADD 7% ONTARIO SALES TAX TO ALL BILLS

EGGS — OMELETTES

ONE SCRAMBLED OR FRIED EGG 1.65
SCRAMBLED OR FRIED EGGS 2.50
POACHED EGGS ON TOAST 2.75
BOILED EGGS 2.50
CHEESE OMELETTE 3.95
SCRAMBED EGGS with Onion 4.00
SCRAMBLED EGGS with Lox 5.30
SCRAMBLED EGGS with LOX and ONIONS 5.95
COTTAGE CHEESE OMELETTE 3.95
BREAD OR BAGEL INCLUDED

CREAM DISHES

BANANAS and SOUR CREAM 2.25
COTTAGE CHEESE WITH CREAM 2.75
VEGETABLE, COTTAGE CHEESE WITH CREAM 3.00
MIXED FRESH FRUIT WITH SOUR CREAM OR YOGURT 3.00
STRAWBERRIES OR BLUEBERRIES
(In Season) with Cream 2.95
BREAD OR BAGEL INCLUDED

DAIRY DISHES

CHEESE BLINTZES 5.00
with Sour Cream or Apple Sauce .75 extra
POTATO PANCAKES (Latkes) (4 large **or** 8 small) 4.75
with Sour Cream or Apple Sauce .75 extra
NOODLES with Cheese and Butter 4.50
BROWN KASHA with Onions 5.00
FARFEL with Beans 4.75
BOILED CHEESE OR POTATO KREPLACH 5.50
KREPLACH (Fried) .50 Extra
with Fried Onions .50
with Sour Cream .75 Extra

FISH

BOILED OR BAKED WHITE FISH 6.95
PICKLED (Sweet and Sour) PIKE 6.95
BAKED CARP 4.25
GEFILTE FISH (Sweet or Peppered) 4.25
FISH with French Fries 5.45
BREAD OR BAGEL INCLUDED

SALADS

PLAIN VEGETABLE 2.75
SALMON or TUNA 6.00   CHOPPED LIVER 6.00
FRESH FRUIT & COTTAGE CHEESE 4.75
COMBINATION 6.50
SARDINE 4.25   BOILED EGG 3.60
CREAM OR COTTAGE CHEESE 4.00
FARMER'S SALAD 4.75
BREAD OR BAGEL INCLUDED

SAN FRANCESCO FOODS

San Francesco Foods, located at 10 Clinton Street below College Street, was the original San Francescos. Opened in 1954, this place was a very small grocery store that sold dry sausages, prosciutto, cured meats, olives and cheeses, and started making sandwiches for takeout. I remember them going through ten to twenty bone-in veal hips a day. These would be cut into cutlets and grindings for sausage meat sauce and meat balls for sandwiches. Peppers would be added for various degrees of heat.

The Monarch House Tavern next door survived only because of San Francescos. I remember when I was a stockbroker in the '60s (five years with Bache and Company), I would get five or six other brokers and get a limo or a taxi and drive up to San Francescos from the financial district. A sandwich back then cost 75 cents, a cup of hot olives 25 cents, and a hunk of great cheese was $1. Draught beer was 25 cents a glass. So for eight small draughts, a large hot veal sandwich with cheese and olives would cost you less than $5; and that included a tip for the waiter. I'm sure the limo or taxi was no more than $5 one way. So, for less than $40, five guys could have a great quick and very filling lunch, go there and come back, and not have to worry about traffic and parking. You could also belch all the way back to work. Those were the days. San Francescos eventually became a franchise operation. This place only closed on Christmas Day and Easter. Down the street and around the corner, a mother and daughter opened the original California Sandwiches. You would think by living in Mississauga in the '60s and '70s, why would my family come to the city to eat so frequently? There were so many great places to eat—why wouldn't we!

PETER PAN

Peter Pan was located at 373 Queen Street West, at Peter Street, and seemed like it was there forever. There had been a restaurant there over 100 years ago and was originally called "The Savoy." In 1936 the Woo family took it over and designated it the Peter Pan.

With its tin ceiling and simple furnishings its ambiance felt like you were in a time warp. It was just east of Barney's, and was home to the hippy generation and coloured hair, somewhat like today. They served very good food and had a fantastic hamburger and varied meats and fish items, and their desserts were second to none. Susur Lee left his footprint here during his brief stay.

Peter Pan Lunch, exterior (1972)

CORNER HOUSE

Hans Kocaurek opened the Corner House in the late '60s at 501 Davenport Road, just below Casa Loma. Hans and his wife ran this operation and it became quite successful. Unfortunately, Hans died far too early in his life. He had been at The Walker House, and I originally met him at the Hyatt Regency, where he moved to with Fred Reindl, the Executive Chef. Peter Kohlberg and his wife bought the Corner House in 1978 and had a successful run as well. Peter brought over many of his popular main course entrées from Winston's, where he was the executive chef. His veal Oscar was a specialty that he created at Winston's, along with beef tenderloin, rack of lamb and duckling items. Soup was served from a large tureen, just like at home. The restaurant was sold again to Herbert Barnsteiner, a chef who worked previously with Mövenpick and his wife. The Barnsteiners announced the closure of the Corner House in February, 2014.

BUMPKIN'S

Bumpkin's was owned and managed by a very charming couple named Connie and Domenico Ciccocioppo. She ran the office, and he ran the dining room. This continental-style restaurant was originally opened at 557 Parliament Street in 1971 and then moved to 21 Gloucester Street, across from Fenton's, in 1979. This was a very popular place both for lunch and dinner and served great home cooked food. The menu was very well priced and gave good value for money spent. Lunch always included soup and salad and was garlic heaven. It was not ostentatious but presented a very comfortable and clean feeling. Patrons would line up outside before they opened (5:30 pm) and the door closed when the place filled up.

As one of my customers, Domenico was always fair. He scrutinized pricing, but always demanded and bought the highest quality, which he later served at Oro (and still does). Steamed lobster and crab legs appeared on the menu. All cuts of red meat, pork, veal and chicken were well represented, and it was an account I wish I had worked more with. This was a place that served great desserts, fruit pies and cheese cakes. Again, you did not have to break the bank when you ate there.

FRAN'S

Fran's tradition started in 1940 at 21 St. Clair Avenue, near Yonge Street by Francis (Fran) Deck and his wife Ellen Jane. It was a modest and very small diner that served simple, fresh, high quality comfort food, such as burgers, chili and rice pudding, and their famous apple pie twenty-four hours a day. It was one of the first "all day" breakfast restaurants in Toronto. Their plate combinations were served from 11 am to 2 am, and their "deck-er" club sandwiches, various hot sandwiches, assorted cold sandwiches, waffles, great coffee, milkshakes and sundaes became famous and won many awards. A hamburger deluxe sold for 25 cents, French fries were 10 cents, and a cup of coffee cost a nickel. Two or three other locations were opened as time went on, but they were closed in due time. They may have been reinvented, but never enjoyed the same success they once did. My favourite location was on Yonge Street near the Ryerson campus, north of Dundas Street. I would enjoy their apple pie and vanilla ice cream during a break from my classes.

Fran Deck with two staff members (ca. 1961-62)

DIANA SWEETS

Originally opened as a candy store at 153 Yonge St in 1912, Diana Sweets eventually expanded to become a restaurant at 187 Yonge Street and was one of the longest established restaurants in Toronto. George Boukydis, a very hands-on owner, was a firm but shy man who was always there. The menu was simple but high-end and classy and catered to City Hall staff, department store executives and shoppers. Their specialty was eggs and salads, and their breakfast and lunch trade was always busy. They were closed on Sundays because of the Sunday liquor laws. Adjoining the restaurant was Joe Bird's bar, a favourite watering hole. The Yonge location closed in 1987.

Diana Sweets, Yonge St. exterior (ca. 1970s)

INDIAN RICE FACTORY

The Indian Rice Factory was opened in 1970 at 414 Dupont Street by Mrs. Amar Patel. The restaurant was quite small and presented a very simple, but inviting, ambiance. Mrs. Patel was the first person to pioneer and lay the groundwork for real discriminating Indian food. She was a very smart and sophisticated woman who cooked first class cuisine. She was very hands on in her business and she placed all of her orders with me. She did all of the cooking herself, and, as Sir Walter Raleigh popularized tobacco, Mrs. Patel popularized curry in Toronto. Indian breads became a specialty as well. As the restaurant progressed, certain wines were married to the different flavours of her food. She bought only top quality meat and chicken products and always said to me that she was buying the same quality from me as the other premier restaurants. Her mother helped with the daily management when she could not handle the load of stress. She died a very proud person, not pretentious or overbearing, as she could have been. Her fingerprints were on the Inn on the Park's Café De L'Auberge, Julie's Mansion on Jarvis in the Bombay Bicycle Club, and then the Hyatt Regency Hotel prior to her opening the Indian Rice Factory. The Indian Rice Factory closed in 2014.

THE PORTS OF CALL

The Ports of Call opened in 1963 at 1145 Yonge Street. Originally the property was the Rosedale Hotel, which became the Northgate Hotel under the ownership of Paul McNamara, who was also Chairman of the Board at Maple Leaf Gardens. Domenic Rubinato was the executive chef at the Northgate, which specialized in steak flambé in their dining room. The Northgate was purchased in the early 1950s and was changed to the Ports of Call in 1963, which consisted of different restaurants. Millions were spent to build this structure because it was built from scratch. There was the Dickens Room, which served English fare in old England's finest hostelry tradition with early 19th century décor and large fireplaces. Caesar's Garden and Grotto was a large dining room that had the atmosphere and opulence of ancient Rome, serving authentic Italian and continental cuisine.

The Last Chance Saloon had a gay '90s atmosphere and was a popular watering hole. The Ballon Rouge was a large, sophisticated cocktail bar with a French atmosphere. The Bali-hi was composed of three different themes: Japanese, Chinese, and Polynesian, and drinks of the South Pacific were served there. These restaurants became very popular on the Toronto restaurant scene, and served as a new beginning for many people working in the hospitality industry. Others moved to jobs that were opening up in the hotel industry, which was growing quickly.

THE BROWN DERBY

The Brown Derby, although it was not known for its culinary offerings, was a great place to imbibe. The large room had an old-time atmosphere and continuous live entertainment from 2 pm to 1 am, except on Sundays; it featured Joe King and the Zaniaks, a comedic singing group. Being centrally located at the corner of Yonge and Dundas, it was a magnet for "funsters." The Gay Nineties Room, calling to mind the decadent and scandalous 1890s, had Sammy Sales as the host for many years, and it offered a sing along and old time silent movies. With a buffet, people could spend the whole day in there. There was no cover charge for the entertainment. Occasionally, topless female bands would perform and the place would be so packed that people would spill out onto the sidewalk. Most cocktails (based on 1 ¼ ounces) Collins-long tails, Flips and Fizzies, Egg Nogs, Sours, imported and Canadian brandies, imported and Canadian rums, liqueurs, rye and scotch and Irish whiskies, were all priced under 80 cents. Wines by the glass were 40 cents. A soft drink was a dime. All these prices included the Ontario Hospital Tax.

The Brown Derby Tavern (1952)
Below: Brown Derby Tavern Cocktail Menu (1961)

ENTERTAINMENT
Menu
The prices shown in this Menu include the Ontario Hospital Tax.

Brown Derby
YONGE · DUNDAS

COCKTAIL
LIST

BROWN DERBY TAVERN
TORONTO
YONGE & DUNDAS STS. · EM. 6-4438

COCKTAILS
All Portions Based on 1¼ Ozs.

Pink Lady, gin, cream, grenadine	.70
Orange Blossom, gin, orange juice, grenadine	.70
Manhattan, rye, Italian vermouth	.70
Martini Sweet, gin, Italian vermouth	.70
Martini Dry, gin, French vermouth	.70
Old Fashioned, rye, bitters, suga, soda	.75
Daiquiri, rum, lemon juice, sugar	.75
Rob Roy, scotch, Italian vermouth	.75
Creme De Menthe Frappai, creme de menthe, crushed ice	.75
Side Car, brandy, cointreau, lemon juice	.85
Stinger, brandy, creme de menthe	.85
Gimlet, gin or rye, lime juice, sugar	.85
Between the Sheets, brandy, rum, lemon juice	.85
Alexander, brandy or gin, creme de cacao and cream	.85
Grasshopper, creme de cacao, creme de menthe, cream	.85
Bloody Mary, vodka, tomato juice, lime juice	.85
Scarlet O'Hara, Southern Comfort, lime juice, grenadine	.85
B. and B., Benedictine, cognac	.90
Champagne Cocktail, champagne, sugar, bitters, lemon twist	1.00
Bacardi, Bacardi rum, lime juice, grenadine	1.05
Poussé Café, grenadine, creme de cacao, anisette, creme de menthe, cointreau, cognac	1.25

COLLINS—LONG TAILS
All Portions Based on 1¼ Ozs.

Tom Collins, gin, lemon juice, sugar, soda	.70
Gin Rickey, gin, lime, soda	.70
Rye Collins, rye, lemon juice, soda, sugar	.75
Brandy Collins, brandy, lemon juice, soda, sugar	.75
Pimm's No. 1 Cup, Pimm's No. 1, Seven-Up	.75
Pimm's No. 5 Cup, Pimm's No. 5, Seven-Up	.75

Rum Collins, rum, lemon juice, sugar, soda	.80
Cuba Libre, rum, lime, coca-cola	.80
Planter's Punch, rum, fruit juice, cointreau, soda	.85
Singapore Sling, gin, fruit juice, cherry brandy, soda	.85
Rum Swizzle, rum, lemon juice, bitters, soda	.85
Moscow Mule, vodka, lime, ginger beer	.85
Screwdriver, vodka, orange juice	.85
Zombie, Jamaican, Barbados, Puerto Rican rums, fruit juice, green creme de menthe	1.70

FLIPS AND FIZZES
All Portions Based on 1¼ Ozs.

Sherry Flip, sherry, egg, sugar	.65
Port Flip, port, egg, sugar	.65
Gin Fizz, gin, lemon juice, soda	.70
Rum Flip, rum, egg, sugar	.75
Sloe Gin Fizz, sloe gin, grenadine, lemon juice, sugar	.75
Silver Fizz, gin, white of egg, lemon juice, sugar	.75
Golden Fizz, gin, egg yolk, lemon juice, sugar	.75
Royal Fizz, gin, egg, lemon juice, sugar	.75
Brandy Flip, brandy, sugar, egg	.75

EGG NOGS
All Portions Based on 1¼ Ozs.

Whiskey Egg Nog, rye, egg, milk, sugar	.80
Brandy Egg Nog, brandy, egg, milk, sugar	.85
Rum Egg Nog, rum, egg, milk, sugar	.85

SOURS
All Portions Based on 1¼ Ozs.

Whiskey Sour, rye, lemon juice, soda	.75
Brandy Sour, brandy, lemon juice, soda	.75
Rum Sour, rum, lemon juice, soda	.80
Scotch Sour, scotch, lemon juice, soda	.85

BRANDIES (CANADIAN)
All Portions Based on 1 Oz.

Paul Masson	.65

GINS (Canadian)
All Portions Based on 1 Oz.

Domestic Gin	.60

Sloe Gin .65

THE ABOVE PRICES INCLU

SORRY WE CANNOT BE RESPONS

500 9-60

The Brown Derby Tavern (1971)

EATON'S AND SIMPSON'S

Both Eaton's and Simpson's are long gone now, but both were my good customers; they provided good value to their customers and businessmen when they lunched there. They competed against each other, but I am sure they shared secrets, being neighbours. Eaton's, with its Georgian Room on the 9th floor, served appetizing cuisine. Simpson's, with its Arcadian Court on the 8th and 9th floors, featured their famous afternoon tea between 2 and 5 pm, which included very fashionable finger sandwiches popular with the ladies. Wedding cakes ordered from the Arcadian Court were very special and very popular in the 50s, 60s and 70s. They were pre-portioned to give as gifts to guests and it saved a lot of work and mess. The Oliver Bonacini Group now operates that room.

MALLONEY'S CHOP HOUSE

Malloney's was located at 85 Grenville Street, next to Napoléon. This was a human 'meet' market that pioneered the stand-up bar scene. This was a haven for advertising executives. Patrons would go in Wednesdays, Thursdays and Fridays to set up their dates for Saturdays and the weekend. It was a singles paradise. Dining was English style chophouse fare, featuring steak, lamb chops, liver and mixed English grill. Sandwiches and stew were served on Saturday. When the restaurant closed for redevelopment, the action moved over to the new Hydro building on University Avenue at College.

JULIE'S MANSION

Who would have thought that the Massey House at 515 Jarvis Street would have become the location of racy Julie's Mansion? The mansion was built in 1868 by Sentaor William McMaster, founder of McMaster University. Hart Massey purchased it in the mid-1880s as a family home, and it became a hospital during World War I for soldiers. In the early '60s, a time when the culture of the Playboy Club was taking off, the mansion turned into Julie's Mansion by Jules Fine; it opened in 1963. Fine, a close friend of Harry Barberian, had started the Gaslight in Yorkville, just a stone's throw away from Joso's and Dinkels (who was our first account at J.J. Derma Meats). With Julie's Mansion, Fine's dreams came true. He hired Mrs. Amar Patel, who gained fame later at her Indian Rice Factory, to cook and formulate menus at the provocative and racy Bombay Bicycle Club, located in the mansion. The waitresses wore sensual saris that attracted the playboy club type of characters. Steaks included New York sirloin, tenderloin, pepper steak and, my favourite, steak tartar. A violinist played throughout the dinner hours in the dining room, which was separate from the Bombay Bicycle Club and had more of a steakhouse venue.

The place was a raving success. I met Rudy Gamper there, a chef who would go on to become the chef of "Trader Vics" in the Hotel Toronto where we did business for years. Rudy was a small person but was very strong in that, when he became angry one day, he buried a cleaver ½ an inch into his wooden chopping block. Wow did he have a temper! After a successful run, the Mansion became the "Keg Mansion" and is still in operation.

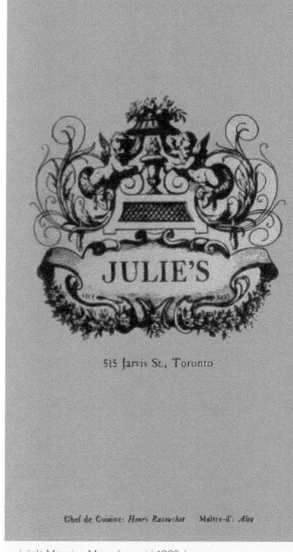

JULIE'S

515 Jarvis St., Toronto

Chef de Cuisine: *Henri Racowhie*   Maître-d': *Alex*

Julie's Mansion Menu (ca. mid-1960s)

THE CHRYSALIS GROUP

The Chrysalis organization started in the early '80s by Tom Kristenbrun (T.K.) and Neil Vosburgh. The properties they owned were Bemelmans, Bellair Cafe (Old Mr. Tony's), Rhodes, The Ports, The Riverside in Oakville, the Jarvis House, and Bistro 990. The Copa was opened after the Ports closed. The Ports had been controlled by Concertina Inc., originally a company owned by Conwest Exploration. Tom Kristenbrun originally co-owned the El Mocombo, The Riverside and Jarvis House. T.K. was the President. Later, the Ascot Inn was bought and turned into a nightclub and entertainment center.

THE UNDERGROUND RAILROAD

The Underground Railroad Restaurant took its name from the secret 19th century network that black slaves used to escape the plantations in the American Deep South. It was opened in 1969 at 225 King Street East by three gentlemen: Archie Alleyne, John Henry Jackson and Howard Matthews. Archie was a jazz drummer who I frequently saw playing at George's Spaghetti House; John Henry was an accomplished athlete who played quarterback for the Toronto Argonauts Football team; and Howard was a man-about-town businessman. This restaurant was the home of 'soul food'. (I had always thought when I was younger that my mother had originated Ukrainian 'soul food'. She would cook stews, fried chicken, boiled and jellied pigs' feet, buckwheat or kasha, okra, squash, cornmeal and her special cornbread called Johnny Cake.) The Underground Railroad would make things like baked ham hocks, pork chitlins, pork tails, stews, fried chicken, ribs, baked ham, steak and gumbo. Gee Mom- you did good! Fresh vegetables such as okra, collard greens, yams, squash and black-eyed peas would make the meals at the Underground quite memorable and delicious. Their hush puppies, corn bread and corn fritters were handed down through generations.

Desserts were heavy, such as sweet potato pie and peach cobbler, but made for excellent home-style fare. Their Anna Mae salad was like a Waldorf, but with added shredded cabbage. Fresh buttermilk was always available, my favourite beverage in the summer. The ambiance was dim and very inviting, with farm-like lanterns, barn board and bare wooden beams. Waiters were dressed in striped railroad bib overalls and necker-chiefs. Sunday brunch was also very popular and I loved it. You really felt like you were in the Deep South. I can't believe that anyone ever left that place underfed.

THE CN TOWER

The top of Toronto, now called 360 The Restaurant at the CN Tower, was opened in 1976 at 301 Front Street West. The restaurant is at the 1000 foot level, although the complete tower is 1815 feet, 5 inches from top to bottom. The restaurant revolves every 72 minutes. Work on the CN Tower went on for 24 hours per day—5 days per week—for 40 months to be completed. Bellwoods Park on Queen Street West was totally filled in from the diggings of the Tower. I remember Bellwoods Park—we would go tobogganing there in the late '40s and early '50s.

When the restaurant opened it had a reservation wait of up to 2 years. This place was my biggest customer ever because of the heavily weighted beef items featured on the original menu. How times have changed! I met the original executive chef, Raymond Locati, who came from Jasper Park Lodge, a CN hotel where I worked in the '60s after I graduated. When I told Raymond about my being at Jasper Park Lodge we connected instantly because he was a total stranger to Toronto. The rest was history. Walter Spaltenstein and Nigel Shute, two executive chefs at the CN Tower in the '70s and '80s, became good friends of my family. Nigel Shute and his good friend Ichi even catered our wedding reception at our home in Lorne Park, Mississauga. Florence and I got married on one of the hottest days of the summer and the large ice sculptures that they created melted quickly. Other chefs manage this restaurant now, and Peter George is the executive chef. One of my regrets is that I did not get to know Mr. George better, but I hope that I will in the future.

IMAGO RESTAURANTS INC.

Once Neil and Tom (see The Chrysalis Group) parted company, Neil started the Imago Group in 1985, which consisted of the Duke of York (on Prince Arthur and previously Glossops), the Duke of Kent (at Yonge and Eglinton), and the Duke of Richmond (at the Eaton Centre). Added later were the Duke of Sommerset and the Duke of Devon. Neil also opened Duncan Street Grill, Pasta on Duncan, the Daily Planet, City Grill, Acme Bar and Grill and Vinnies on Adelaide. R.P.M (on the lake) became another one of his priorities. These were all very heady properties which were very popular on the Toronto dining scene.

TOBY'S GOOD EATS

Toby's was actually begun before Chrysalis was formed. Martin Connell, Alan Venebles and Isobel Beveridge opened the first Toby's Good Eats, which evolved into The Chrysalis Group. Martin Connell later started the Ace Bakery, which was quite a successful venture. The original Toby's was opened at 93 Bloor Street West and grew up to a total of 12 properties at the height of their popularity. Sandblasted brick walls and lots of greenery provided a very accommodating and friendly atmosphere. Great hand cut chunky fries, delicious burgers accompanied by shakes, sodas, beer and wine, made these places extremely popular. Parking and deliveries on Bloor Street during all the wrong times became a real challenge. My trucks would be towed frequently with the meat products still inside them. Quite a laugh now, but it certainly was not then!

Jody Ortved (now passed on), became a good friend. He started at the Jarvis House, worked at The Ascot and The Ports, and started at Toby's in 1981 where I got to know him. He became an operating partner and ran the operation until the late '90s. In 2008 we reconnected.

CHARACTERS

GREG COUILLARD

Many things have been written about Greg and his associations with various restaurants. I have supplied some of them in the 1980s and '90s, but I must say I have never been hurt financially. I had to chase after the money, but never got stiffed. I was very lucky.

Greg was always a gentleman towards me, and I felt very comfortable dealing with him and his various associates and co-workers. When he was on, he was brilliant. When the dark side took over, he lost it. He was never a formally trained Chef, nor did he have any training in the culinary business. He could create magic with what he had to work with. He worked hard and had incredible imagination to do the things he accomplished. On his life adventure in the food business, he loved New York City and stayed there for a year. That is where he seriously decided to be a chef and returned to Toronto in 1982 to work as a night chef at Emilio's, a New York kind of bistro.

A few years went by until 1986 when I became his main meat supplier at Stelle, a restaurant on Queen Street West near Bathurst. I loved Stelle, and that is where I really got to work with Greg and appreciate his talents. His apartment at this time was on Queen Street West at Ryerson Avenue. I used to live at Ryerson Avenue and Wolseley Street, just behind and across the laneway from Greg's place. My family owned a grocery store there in the 1940s. When I looked out of Greg's back window on the third floor, I could see what used to be my family's backyard. The grocery store was replaced by a row of low-cost housing units. I visited him there to pick up weekly cheques that were outstanding on his meat purchases. Stelle was a very 'in and hot' place, seating only about thirty with no warm ambiance; it was retro and very busy for a small place. It was here at Stelle that Greg cultivated his reputation. He cooked there for a period of three years.

The next step for Greg was Oceans with Charles Kabouth. It was a mismatch, in that Oceans was too hectic and turned into 'a circus'. I dealt with Charles Kabouth for a short period and I doubt that he would even remember me. He paid all outstanding financial obligations to me, so I had no quarrel with him. I believe I dealt with his father briefly, who worked with his son. Oceans subsequently closed in 1991, leaving a bad taste in the mouths of its suppliers.

China Blue was the next stop. It was on King Street East. I remember the 'opening'. The place was packed like sardines in a can. My friend, Bill Ballard, was there, along with a great actor and the heart-throb of my wife, Florence, Christopher Plummer. It was certainly a night to be remembered. The place closed a year later and reopened for a short time, but closed for good in 1992. I had enough and my luck ran out. I did not hear from or see Greg for a while. His time at Avec, Trixie, Hudson, Notorious, Sonoma, Couillard's and Magic passed me by.

However, there was another stop for me and Greg called Sarkis on Richmond Street East, just east of Church Street. Greg and Sarkis Tossounian (owner) won me over and I was 'all in' again. This time, I got to know Sarkis, the money man. All went well because I was paid weekly and never had any problems. Greg created a new menu and the place was fabulous. I actually enjoyed my involvement with Greg and Sarkis because there was "no bullshit." However, the place closed and my association with Greg unfortunately came to an end. In the past he would bring up Costa Rica and hoped to open up a place down there. He asked me if I was interested but I was involved in my business, which was doing well. I don't know if he ever went after that dream. He seemed to disappear from the restaurant scene, but I do wish him success in anything he does. He was truly a character of the '70s, '80s and '90s on the Toronto restaurant scene.

MICHAEL STADLTLÄNDER

Michael arrived in Toronto in 1980, but I did not meet him until 1982 at the Rosedale Diner over a cup of coffee. We discussed the meat business and I really felt that he was feeling me out and seeing if I was going to be of service to his needs. He was a different kind of cat. I could feel that he was someone who would become very special, and I welcomed him into my world.

Michael secured a chef position at the controversial 21 McGill, a private Ladies Club. He called me one day and said that the club was having its Grand Opening, and he needed one hundred tenderloins for the event. Now that was a nice order. We were in a recession, but Michael quoted Isobel Beveridge as saying, 'there's no recession at 21 McGill.' The tenderloin went in and Michael created a fabulous meal, but a few months later the club went bankrupt. Needless to say, I paid for a great culinary evening! After the announcement was made, my friend Harold Ballard threatened to buy the place and turn it into a "Playboy Club." What a riot that would have caused!

In 1984, Michael opened Stadtländers on John Street just north of Queen Street. I remember the kitchen was like a small, tight bowling lane with not much refrigeration space. Daily deliveries did not present a problem for long, because the restaurant closed shortly after.

Although our ticket into the restaurant trade was procuring offal for discriminating menus, Michael introduced a lot of diners to these products. My association with Michael was curtailed because he went to 100% organic in meats, fruits and vegetables. There was no room for me because we were not into organic. A lot of the organic-sourced meat products were not federally inspected, so we could not participate in that trade. I know that Michael was involved with Nekah (with T.K.) and Knives and Forks. Organic farming had taken root and a revolutionary movement in the culinary world in Toronto had started.

Michael and his wife Nobuyo tried to find their place in the sun and travelled to Europe and the west coast of British Columbia, but never felt more comfortable anywhere outside of Ontario. The Stadtländers finally found their home in Singhampton and called it Eigensinn Farm. Most ingredients and products they used in their cooking came from the farm or locals. I am sorry that I could not participate in Michael's journey, but I had no control over that. I met Michael at an Escoffier function some years ago, and he looked very happy and satisfied. In 2002 he was named the Ninth Best Chef in the World by London Restaurant Magazine.

JOHN MAXWELL

John Maxwell could be described as "a New York kind of guy." I originally met him at Joe Allen's on John Street, near where the Toronto International Film Festival building now stands. He was always very well dressed and was very cool and composed. He could have walked out of a *Gentleman's Quarterly* magazine. I loved the silver star in his front tooth. I got to know John better when he ran Orso, on John Street and Adelaide. He would tell me about his collection of Jaguars, which I became interested in and ultimately became an owner of one.

Orso became a very popular place, where you could smoke a great Cuban cigar and nobody would give you a second look. Our family had a few great parties there. The place was so accommodating, but it was he who really made the place. Later, John struggled through tight times and ultimately wound up on the Danforth, at Allen's on the Danforth. He has been settled there for almost thirty years and has become an integral part of that area.

AL CARBONE

From the first day I met Al Carbone, I instantly liked him. I met Al in 1989 through a mutual friend of ours—Bill Ballard—who owned the building next door to Al's and Cathy Horvath's Confectionary Store and Sandwich Shop, which later became the Kit Kat Restaurant. Bill Ballard and Al were close friends and neighbours, and Bill invited me in to speak to Al about helping him out with supplying him with meat products. That turned out to be very rewarding. Al was an accommodating and quiet business man, always analyzing things so that he could learn and manage his business better. He always stood up for what he thought, and would never take the easy way out of situations. We had our moments. I have never seen him in a suit, but always very casually dressed, often in a bulky, comfortable, cardigan sweater. The clothes really matched the man's personal nature.

His restaurant- the Kit Kat- mirrored Al's character, simplistic yet very cool. The Kit Kat became a celebrity hang out, and Al and Cathy treated celebrities like family, and they felt like they were at home. Al got some of his early training in the business at the Royal York, where he was a waiter under the tutelage of another mutual friend, Louis Jannetta. The restaurant was very home-like, yet chic and trendy. I will never forget the black cat mascot, 'Kitty Kat', with his tiny black bowtie patrolling the restaurant. He stuck around for fourteen years. The Mediterranean inspired food was quite satisfactory and the selections varied. Over the years, I dealt with different chef personalities like Freddie Lo Cicero and Fern Poudrette (Fingers). Raffaello Ferrari passed through very briefly, while Ravi Anandappa stayed the longest, and is still there.

Freddy always asked me if I had anymore water buffalo to sell. I guess he must have got a tough steak, but he was very sarcastic and funny. When he passed away, I missed him.

LOUIS JANNETTA

Louis Jannetta arrived in Toronto in 1935 at the age of seven. He started as a busboy at the Royal York Hotel in 1942, and graduated through the years to become the Maître d' and Manager of the Black Knight Room in 1962. Louis probably met as many, or more, celebrities than Mr. Hans Gerhardt did at the Sutton Place Hotel. When we used to meet after Louis retired, he told me hundreds of stories, and his book, King of the Maître d's, provided many more about his life at the Royal York and gives a detailed account of his trials and tribulations.

Louis opened Louis Jannetta's Place in 1994. There were countless memento pictures of Louis' life at the Royal York of all of the celebrities that visited. He really did meet many famous performers, such as Frank Sinatra, Ella Fitzgerald, Pavarotti, Ginger Rogers and Marlene Dietrich. Tony Bennett became a very close friend of his. Louis worked late and long hours to promote the restaurant, but was too good to his employees, who took advantage of him. When I delivered in the mornings there was always an item missing by the time the chef arrived. Louis couldn't spend twenty-four hours a day there. It became too much to deal with. His good nature hurt him in the end, and the restaurant had to close in 1999.

His crowning moment however, was seeing and hearing his daughter Patti perform in the Imperial Room at The Royal York. Louis regretted, more than anything, his lack of time spent with his wife and family. You could see it at his funeral viewing in 2013. Hundreds and hundreds of photos with his wife, Coreen, and family along with a very proud Louis in the middle. He always mentioned his family. His heart was in the right place. He started, and supported, the Italian Canadian Hockey Association for almost fifty years. He was invested as a Knight of Malta for this charitable work and was involved in Variety Village. Louis lived in his special era of glamour and elegance. He truly was the 'King of Maître ds'.

ALBERT OLIVA

Albert Oliva was a Hollywood-type character who reminded me of George Raft. He smoked large cigars and drank Chivas Regal scotch whiskey. I was honoured to know him, as he was one of the important builders of the Whaler's Wharf organization, which was also an important customer of J.J. Derma Meats. Albert's early days involved work with his brother-in-law in the auto body industry, and developing a company called Alton Truck Body, which became very successful. He ventured into the construction business, which led him to be involved in the construction of a strip plaza project on Dundas at Wharton Way in Mississauga. A restaurant was supposed to be part of the project, but it did not happen. Albert and his team took over the restaurant and the Whalers Wharf Organization was begun. Walter Oster and Marcello Gasparetto joined Albert and added Pier 4 to the three Whaler's Wharf locations, and, later on, the Admiral Hotel on the waterfront as well. This was not Albert's first restaurant attempt, as he was the successful owner of the Sir Nicholas Restaurant on Roncesvalles Avenue, which was a popular venue for Polish and Ukrainian weddings, anniversaries and other social functions.

A favourite memory of mine in regards to Albert was when he would invite me to come over for lunch. The lunch would not be at one of his restaurants, but at the auto body shop where he would have fresh cold cuts, cheeses and dill pickles accompanied by fresh rye bread. Albert would have a shot of Chivas and I would have a cold beer. What a simple-living kind of guy. He loved the sport of kings, horse racing, and was at the track frequently. He did enjoy life and sadly passed away too early.

VERY HONOURABLE MENTIONS

I'm sure there were many favourite eating experiences in the last sixty years that I have not mentioned. It would take a book of at least one thousand pages to report all those places. However, there are a few that stand out.

In the '50s and '60s there was a great place to go 'necking' with your girlfriend called Brookers. It was located on the present site of the Palace Pier condominiums beside the Humber River. You could shine your headlights and watch the rats scuffle across the Lake Ontario shoreline at night while you ate a twelve inch hotdog. But the main reason was still to exercise your neck. The current street, a short thoroughfare called Brookers' Lane, is a reminder today of those great times.

Just west and down the street was the Pickin' Chicken Bar-B-Q, which was like the present day Swiss Chalet. The Pickin' Chicken had only six locations but served the best barbecued chicken ever. Their sauce was to die for. Their other five locations were on Queen Street West at Roncesvalles, on Kingston Road in the east end of Toronto, on Weston Road, at Bathurst and Finch, and on Bayview at Millwood. They were all open from 10:30 AM to 2:00 AM daily. When I worked at Swift and Company, we supplied all of the chicken out of our Burlington chicken plant. Sammy, the chef, always kept me well supplied with their famous BBQ sauce. The sauce came in forty ounce cans, so you can imagine how much BBQ sauce we used. I caught up with Sammy years later at the Whalers Wharf where he was a chef.

Stoodleigh's had a location in the *Toronto Star* building on Yonge Street and another at the Canadian National Exhibition. The location at the CNE served a great cut of roast prime rib and was packed during the Exhibition's Grand Stand shows. Swift and company also supplied the beef.

Lindy's was a place that served the cheapest steak (under $2) in Toronto, and served tons of it weekly. As you passed by on Yonge Street at Gerrard you could smell the marinade used in tenderizing those steaks. However, regardless of the smell, it was a very popular place to frequent. Not everyone could afford to go to a premium steakhouse.

Just down the street was Bassel's on the corner of Gerrard and Yonge Street. Bassel's gave many new immigrants their first start in the restaurant business, who then went on to bigger and better things. They were also benefactors of the Maple Leaf Gardens post game hockey crowd.

The Queen City Lunch at Queen and Bathurst served as a second home to my father, John, and I.

With John spending long hours at his business, the Lucky Strike Cigar Store, the Queen City provided many lunches and dinners. This place never specialized in anything, but everything. It was never empty or slow.

Trader Vic's was a Polynesian themed restaurant that was opened in the Hotel Toronto on Richmond Street at University Avenue. My good friend, Rudy Gamper, was the chef at Trader Vic's, and had come over from Julie's Mansion on Jarvis Street. It became a very popular place and served quite a distinctive menu that featured over seventy five entrées. When they cooked their meats, they hung the product on hooks over heat in a clay-type cooking oven. Various luscious alcoholic drinks were served in a colourful Polynesian, rattan furnished, motif. It was always a fun place to go.

I conducted business at The Tops, The Saxony, The Superior and The Silver Rail, all within a stone's throw of each other on Yonge Street. Thank goodness my delivery trucks could stop in the laneways behind these restaurants to deliver their orders. They were heady days.

I am also happy to say that J.J. Derma Meats, at one time, supplied the prestigious Executive Dining Rooms of the Canadian Imperial Bank of Commerce, the Royal Bank and the Bank of Montreal. The executive dining rooms were for the bank and their preferred guests only. Security was very tight, and when I visited the chefs at these places it was like trying to get into Fort Knox. Who would want to hurt or kill any of these bank executives? It was a very paranoid experience. The chefs at these places spared no expense in buying food products for these executives. Food cost was not an issue. Nothing was too good for them. After all, they did control the Canadian economy, and so their secret business deals were made in their own backyards.

Along with supplying the big Canadian banks, J.J. Derma also had customers at many of the prestigious private clubs, such as the Albany Club, the University Club, National Club, Granite Club, Toronto Club, Royal Canadian Military Institute Club, Boulevard Club, Toronto Club, Board of Trade Country Club, Royal Canadian Yacht Club, Island Yacht Club and Port Credit Yacht Club. These private clubs were sanctuaries for young corporate executives, and were a very significant 'perk' for those who could secure membership. At one time you could become a member of a private club and a golf and country club, but in the last twenty years things have changed. The private clubs have lost their appeal to executives and being a member of a prestigious golf club has taken precedence. Membership in these private clubs has declined and become a real problem. Many of the old members have retired or passed away and younger executives don't have the interest in private club culture. Food costs have become an issue and the quality of food has suffered.

SHOULD-A, WOULD-A, COULD-A

There are regrets in a person's life that, when you really think about them, they aren't major regrets because of the other positive things that have been accomplished. When I was graduating from Ryerson in May of 1965, I had already secured a job at Jasper Park Lodge in Alberta. The job was a position of Staff and Payroll Supervisor, newly created so that I could get to know all positions at the Lodge and recommend how to make them better. I had the complete season, from May to September, to accomplish this. Jasper Park Lodge was only open during the summer season at that time. Being hired in the Special Management Training Program, I was expected to move along to another Canadian National Hotel in the Fall-Winter season and then return to Jasper the next summer.

I was hired by Mr. Ted Vandyke and he said great things were expected of me, so I had to work hard. At Jasper I met George McCabe and Jean Deadman, who were later married. George was in the Front Office Reservations Department working with Jean. This was a very important position that involved booking conventions and tours, which were the bread and butter of the Lodge's business. He later enjoyed a very rewarding career with CN Hotels. He served as General Manager at The Besborough Hotel in Saskatoon, and finally took a position as General Manager of the Congress Centre in Ottawa.

Premier Ernest Manning of the Social Credit Party in Alberta was a frequent guest at Jasper Park Lodge with his family. His son Preston later became Premier and started the Reform Party in Canada. He could have been a Prime Minister of Canada.

Moving forward, the summer came to an end and my next assignment was to be a Food and Beverage Trainee at the Hotel Newfoundland in St. John's. What a thought! My spending the winter in Newfoundland—how could that be? It was then my father, John, was told that he had Tuberculosis. That's all I had to know. My mother, Mary, convinced me to not go on with the CN program and stay in Toronto. My hotel aspirations were over.

In the meantime I have a great story about that Jasper summer. My job as Staff and Payroll Supervisor required me to work a split shift, meaning that I worked from 6:00 am to 11:00 am, and then 6:00 pm to 11:00 pm. That meant I had every afternoon off to do what I wanted. I began to play golf daily and visit my friend and Executive Chef, Marcel Peron, at the Club House. He allowed me to eat lunch there frequently. I also got to know the golf pro, Ron McLeod. What a great life! One day I was asked to play with a pretty good golfer. His name was the Reverend Billy Graham. Hanging around the Pro Shop, I was asked to play with visiting guests to help make up a foursome, but to play with the Reverend was something very special. I accepted and was literally overwhelmed. I shanked my first shot. My reaction was to swear and say, 'God damn it!' The Reverend, who was also a 'scratch golfer' said, 'Ronald, please do not use the Lord's name in vain, and if you do, you will be removed as my golf partner'. Billy Graham played golf with Bob Hope, Bing Crosby and other famous celebrities, so it was a special treat to be with him. When he gave his evangelical preaching's in Edmonton and Calgary, he frequently visited Jasper Park Lodge.

I was still a young man and Heaven only knows what awaited me in the hotel business. I imagined many times the glorious life of a hotel manager, but I always came back to reality. I am so thankful that I had two wonderful children from my first wife, which would not have been possible if I had stayed in the hotel business.

REGRETS

Everyone has regrets in their life. I have many, both in my private and business lives. I won't talk about my private regrets, but here are some of my business regrets:

1. Not getting to know Albino Silva better. I met him briefly when he was with the Whaler's Wharf organization in the 1980s, but I did not follow up to create a closer friendship. I was younger and he was very much younger. He was a charming and very nice person. I know I could have helped in some way as a supplier, and maybe as a friend. I wonder if he remembers me? With the people I did not connect with, I stayed at arms' length. In some cases I really never made an attempt to close the gap and that was a mistake. If only one could relive those times. Albino had his hand in many fine restaurants and added a lot to the Toronto culinary scene.

2. Not getting to know Herbert Sonzogni earlier in his life when he created so many wonderful recipes of success for the Windsor Arms Hotel, the Westbury Hotel, Noodles, the Millcroft Inn and Babsi's. Herbert Sonzocni arrived in Toronto in 1960 at twenty-five years of age. He was offered his first job at the Walker House, but took a job at the Westbury Hotel instead. He stayed for five years and left in 1965. He joined the Windsor Arms Hotel in 1966 and stayed until 1975. In 1975 he went up to the Millcroft Inn (a property of George Minden's of the Windsor Arms Hotel), and stayed until 1981. Herbert and his wife opened a small restaurant in Lorne Park (where I lived) and called it Babsi's. This was when I finally got to know him as a friend and not only as a supplier. The pressure was off him there and he could spend the days working with his wife, which, had been his dream. What a joy to have a place like that in my own backyard. When they sold Babsi's and moved up to Hillsburg my wife and I were already up in Erin. We were practically neighbours. At sixty-one, Herbert bought a farm and cultivated apples for the local restaurant trades. He took his job very seriously, but in 2012 Herb passed away. A kinder and more gentle man like Herbert Sonzogni would be very hard to find.

3. The passing away of Jeremy Brown, a food critic and radio personality that I was getting to know. He was becoming very popular and very easy to listen to. We became friends and conversed frequently. He was a jovial and very friendly person. He died way too early and I wish I could have known him much longer as we could have accomplished a lot together. We had a common interest: he wanted to know about the meat business and I wanted to know more about the restaurant business. I loved his bow ties.

4. Not getting to know Peter Oliver and Michael Bonacini better. My partner and friend, Joe Dermastja, knew Peter Oliver in the early '70s when they were neighbours. I met Peter once, but Joe did all the business with him when he had Oliver's Old Fashioned Bakery and Bofinger. I did get to know Michael a little more. I met him when he first became the Chef at the Windsor Arms. Michael was brought up in Pembrokeshire Wales and his favourite dish was shepherd's pie made from lamb. He came from The Dorchester in London, England, and was very young. I remember him as a quiet,

poised, mild mannered young man who had a lot of responsibility piled on him; he had a lot to prove, what with George Gurnon and Herbert Sonzogni proceeding him. There was a tradition at the Windsor Arms that he was expected to carry on. He gave me a chance as a supplier and I was very grateful for that trust. As time went on, Michael went on his way in the Toronto restaurant scene, becoming a co-chef at Centro and a partner of Jump and Canoe with Peter Oliver. Michael and Peter drove this machine into the conglomerate that it is today. Peter and Michael also had the great foresight to hire both Todd Clarmo and Anthony Walsh as major participants in the most important culinary decisions that the organization made. My son, Tim, took over all dealings with the organizations in the early '90s and maintains good relationships with them to this day. I met Michael at a retirement party for Uli Herzig at the Prince Hotel, and Michael still remembered the first day that I came to call on him at the Windsor Arms. He said, 'Ron, I remember that you had a bright yellow raincoat on." Man that made me feel good that he would remember!

5. Not getting to know Franco Prevedello better. From the time he arrived in Montreal to start his career at Expo 67 to moving through hotel positions in the late '60s, Franco Prevedello moved around like a speeding bullet. While I did the Waltz, Franco was doing the Jitterbug. That is the analysis that I use when he was doing his thing in the restaurant business. This man could not go slowly, going like a treadmill at its maximum speed, and he survived. I met him at the Trillium, Ontario Place, when he was working for John Arena. However, I dealt with the chef and only saw Franco on a few occasions. He was a creator and a brilliant forecaster of what and why a restaurant could succeed. All of the restaurants he opened were successful, although he sold them all. He became bored and was constantly on the lookout for new restaurant ventures. His fingerprints were on so many places. I was too busy with my business to catch up with him, and frankly, I don't know if I could have kept up with his pace and emotions. You may not have liked him, but you had to respect him. He succeeded because he loved himself—which, I think, is the most important characteristic in a person's life. He was not afraid to fail. I am so regretful that I did not stick a rocket up my ass to chase him. I know my son serviced a few of his restaurants, but I regret that I did not join the pursuit.

6. Not getting to know Jamie Kennedy, John Higgins, Keith Froggett, Susur Lee, Marc Thuet, Didier Leroy, Chris Klugman, Mark McEwan and Chris McDonald better. They all left their notable and distinctive hallmarks on the culinary face of Toronto dining. They each have their own story, and I'm just sorry that I could not be a part of it.

EPILOGUE

As time has passed and many restaurants have opened and closed, many of the industry's biggest players have passed on as well. There are not many restaurants that have survived after twenty-five years. Many in this hospitality industry have tried to re-invent the wheel, but, honestly, simplicity and consistency still reign. Anyone who opens a restaurant and serves good food for good value will succeed. Customers are becoming more knowledgeable about the food they consume, more so now than they were in the past; more people understand quality and are willing to pay for it. Of course, hard work and sufficient funding are the most important aspects of business success.

Don't ever question the mentality of your customers, because, if they don't trust you, you may never get another chance to do business with them. Get-rich-quick schemes are becoming less common, although people still stay awake at night trying to dream up new schemes. The introduction of the big American food service distributors to Canada, which were not around twenty-five years ago, have changed the marketplace significantly, but I believe that there will always be a place for the so-called smaller distributors. Hopefully they will succeed, because there is merit in relationships that have been developed over the years. From one meatman to another, I wish you good luck and future success to those meatmen who have survived.

ACKNOWLEDGEMENTS

Thank-you to everyone who had a hand in the making of this book. Thank-you to my family, Florence, Tim, and especially to my daughter, Robin, who was kind enough to do all of the typing for me in the initial stages of writing. Also, special thanks to Rebecca Griffith for reading and typing; I do not have rapid or proficient typing skills and I am eternally grateful to both of them for their assistance. Thank-you to Angelo Fernandes, Peter Hackenberger, Ted Herriott, Walter Hryciuk, Ricardo Roque and Norman Tomas for their support and editorial advice, as well as to everyone who lent me research assistance and shared their stories and knowledge regarding the industry: Arron and Helen Barberian, Waldemar J. Bryk, Tony Calogera, Mary Lyn Campbell, Harry Cardiakos, Connie and Domenic Ciccocioppo, Pearse Dolan, Joe Figliomeni, Francis Fernandes, Brian Goldberg, Jim Gregory, Casey Irvine, Nick Loizou, Klaus Mueller, George McCabe, John Mastroianni, Ed Pietras, Leo and Shirley Spralja, Ken Stathakis, George Skandalakis, Michael Stadtländer, Ted and Helen Traiforos, Louis Janetta, Wolfgang Herget, Athanasios Karamanos, Chris Tripodi, Gordon Wheatley, George Wilson, Neil Vosburgh, William Zilinek and Domenic Zoffranieri. I could not have written this book without you.

IMAGE CREDITS

All images included in this book, unless otherwise stated below, are from the collection of Ronald Chapchuk, or were provided with permission to reproduce from each restaurant/restaurant owner (copyright holder).

The following images are ©Ontario Jewish Archive and were provided with the permission to reproduce:

Page18 (bottom):
Switzer's Delicatessen, Spadina Ave., Toronto, 1974. Ontario Jewish Archives, item 273.

Page 19 (top):
Dick Shatto and Lou Agasee at Shopsy's Restaurant, Spadina Ave., Toronto, 26 October 1961. Ontario Jewish Archives, item 5023.

Page 114 & 115 (in order):
Rose Lieberman, Rose [Hanford?] Green and Aaron and Sarah Ladovsky in front of United Bakers restaurant, Spadina Ave., Toronto, 1920. Ontario Jewish Archives, item 3505.
United Bakers Dairy Restaurant slides, 15 August 1986. Ontario Jewish Archives, fonds 83, file 11.
United Bakers Dairy Restaurant menu, 1986. Ontario Jewish Archives, fonds 83, file 8.

The following images were provided with the kind permission to reproduce from John Chuckman and are ©John Chuckman Archive:

Pages 26 (bottom), 28, 41, 106 (bottom right), 125 (top)

The following images are provided by Toronto Public Archives and are ©City of Toronto unless otherwise stated:

Page 33 & 46:
Windsor Arms Hotel, 1974-75. Fonds 68, File 119.

Page 40 (top):
Savarin Restaurant, west side of Bay Street and Adelaide Street. Fonds 1118, Series 377, Item 457.

Page 54 (top):
Harold Ballard of the Toronto Maple Leafs Hockey Club, with Miss Tiger Cat and Miss Blue Bomber, 196?. Fonds 1257, Series 1057, Item 2409.

Page 67:
View of Harry's Steak House on Church Street at Maitland Street, June 15 1971. Fonds 1526, File 8, Item 30.

Page 68:
Sign of the Steer Restaurant, 1955. Fonds 1257, Series 1057, Item 504.

Page 72:
Carman's Restaurant, Alexander Street, 1973. Fonds 1118, Series 377, Item 809.

Pages 82 and 83:
Valhalla Inn (ca. 1960-1969). Fonds 261, Series 1148, File 50.

Page 87:
Old Angelo's, Yonge Street and Elm Street. Fonds 200, Series 1465, File 20, Item 35.

Page 104:
Walker House Hotel, 1970. Fonds 1118, Series 377, Item 164.

Page 117:
Peter Pan Lunch, July 12, 1972. Fonds 1118, Series 377, Item 464

Page 119:
Fran Deck, 1961-62. Fonds 2, Series 8, File 254.

Page 119:
Diana Sweets, Yonge Street, June 23, 1970-July 25, 1984. Fonds 1526, File 4, Item 18.

Page 122:
The Brown Derby Tavern at Yonge and Dundas Street, 1952. Fonds 1128, Series 381, File 210, Item 9820-2.

Page 123:
The Brown Derby Tavern at Yonge and Dundas Street, 1971. Fonds 1526, File 4, Item 2.

INDEX